RECOVERING THROUGH THE PSALMS

DAVID LaPLANTE

David LaPlante

Recovering Through The Psalms

Copyright © 2016 David LaPlante

All Scripture references are from the Authorized Version (King James Version), unless otherwise noted.

ISBN-13: 978-1523920242
ISBN-10: 1523920246

Introduction

Spending my entire life as an agnostic, I learned to reap the rewards of living without accountability. As an agnostic, I got to sit on the fence, as life passed me by, never truly fearing any repercussions, other than those imposed by my fellow man and society's laws. God was the least of my worries. To me, there was always a slim chance that He existed; and, even if He did, then I would cross that bridge when I got there. I was my own higher power. I alone guided my life, and I earned every gift I had received. Every accomplishment, every gain I made, was by my doing alone. I was right about all of it. All of it except that God <u>WAS</u> there, watching and waiting.

Through it all, I <u>GAINED</u> a disease.

I <u>ACCOMPLISHED</u> becoming an alcoholic.

And I reaped the repercussions, heaped high upon my plate.

I was hopeless and lost; but not forgotten. I struggled for many years as an alcoholic. Even in my youth, while my life was still manageable, when I drank, I did so alcoholically. I had no control over alcohol's effects on me. In my late twenties, my addiction morphed into the monster that made my life unmanageable. I volunteered for a deployment to the Middle East, trying to escape my demons. I spent an entire year in Kuwait, dry and sober. I felt better. I felt like I once again had control. And I came home to a relieved family, who saw me once again healthy and happy.

A few short months is all it took to revert to my old ways. My life had again become unmanageable, and the bottle was all that I craved. In desperation, I had checked myself into more hospitals than I care to admit. There was nearly no psychiatric ward in the state where they did not know my name. In the course of less than 3 years, I completed nine separate 30-day in-patient rehabs, and one 90-day, as well. I finally got it. As of March 18th, 2013 I was sober. I lived in AA for the first large chunk of my sobriety, attending daily meetings, sometimes up to three a day. The desperation that brought me into the rooms and kept me sober, however, was never enough to challenge my agnosticism. I was so firmly rooted in my beliefs that even death itself could not topple the structure. You NEED a higher power in recovery, and mine was the fellowship. They tell you that that is okay in recovery. The big book even has a chapter dedicated to it, called "We Agnostics". I stayed sober for two and a half years this way.

They say that the farther you get from your last drink, the closer you get to your next one. I hated that saying. I was never going to drink again. I was strong in my new-found way of life, and I could not be moved.

Until that day came.

I was on my way home from work, stressed and lonely. I decided that I was above my old ways, and had finally earned that drink. I stopped at the package store and bought a pint. That first sip tasted like pure guilt. It tasted so good; but I awoke, three weeks later, in the hospital, in disbelief of where I had gone, and all of the damage that was done in such a short time.

Yet, it wasn't enough to get me to stop. I reached out for help, and when it came, I pushed it away. Several hospital stays later, I finally reached out to someone I hadn't before. I thought it was just a person; but, in fact, it was God.

I had worked the last two years with a man whom I had known to be very religious. He was religious to the point where I tried to be mindful of my actions around him, out of respect for his faith. I silently thought of him as a fool, just as I thought of all of those who believed in a divine presence. I had judged him through my telescope of self-righteousness. In my desperation to simply not die, I reached out to this man; and he came to me without hesitation. He brought food to fill my empty cupboards, and words to soothe my suffering. He continued to come, even though I did not put down the drink. He brought his wife, and together, they sat with me in my drunken stupor, and prayed for me. They blessed my house and asked the Lord to watch over me. I did not put down the drink. In the hospital, for the fourth time in three months, they came to visit me each day. They brought me a Bible, and literature to try and introduce me to the Lord. I see now that this is where the seed had been planted. However, it did not flower yet. I left the hospital, and this man and his wife took me into their home. I had to give up the apartment, because I had not paid rent since I had relapsed. They fed me, bought me a bed, and gave me a room to call my own; and they suggested I read the Bible. They didn't push, but simply suggested. And I put down the drink for a short while.

Self pity brought me back to alcohol. I began to drink again, and hide it from my friends. After all, I had lost so much that I deserved to bury my sorrows. In late January, I checked myself into a hotel and went on a self-destructive journey that ultimately ended in a brief moment of clarity. I called out to the man and his wife for help, because I knew I was dying. They were there instantly, and swept me back up. No judgment, no scolding, no scoffing. I needed to detox in a hospital, and spent four days in the intensive care unit; after which, they welcomed me back into their home, and told me how good it felt to have me back. No judgment. I can't exactly explain what happened over the next couple days. God works in mysterious ways sometimes. I realized I was living in a holy place. I was surrounded by books upon books of the holy Word. Every crevice of this home was dedicated to the Lord, and it was now my home. Like a light switch being thrown, I was struck with the urge to read the Word.

I walked into the kitchen where the man and his wife sat, and said "I feel like reading. Any suggestions?" They pondered for a moment, and finally, she said, "Read Psalm 119". So I did. A short while later she said I should write what I have interpreted from the reading. I cracked a joke about being back in college, and broke out my pad and a pen. I was shocked how freely the words flowed from me onto paper. There was clearly something working through me, feeding my fingers to move and scribe. It was GOD! I found it so therapeutic that I asked for another "assignment". After completing that one the man, an accomplished author, suggested that I take each of the Psalms, one by one, and write about them; and then to even organize it into a book. A book?! I was no author. He offered to help, so I began to write. I would give him each one as they were completed, and, before I knew it, this book began to take form! God was creating this book through me!

Scott and Jacqui Testori had introduced me to God ever so kindly and gently, and now I was creating in His presence. Scott asked me what I wanted to title the book, and I told him I want it to be about recovery. I wanted to create something that could help the still-suffering addicts and alcoholics. My interpretations of the Psalms in relation to my story do not require you to know the Psalms, or even, for that matter, to believe in God. This is a message of hope and joy, as I revel in sobriety. I pray that God will help me to deliver His message in a manner that even the agnostic or the atheist can hear; for they are my brothers, too, and I do not judge. May this be a kind and gentle introduction to the Lord, much like the one I was given. But whether you are a believer or not, still, know that there is hope. I found mine in the Lord.

David Laplante

Saturday, January 30, 2016

Fear thou not; for I am with thee:

be not dismayed; for I am thy God:

I will strengthen thee;

yea, I will help thee;

yea, I will uphold thee with the right hand

of my righteousness.

(Isaiah 41:10)

Psalm 1

The first Psalm speaks to me in a way which I feel I've needed to hear for a long time. If I walk the path of righteousness, I shall not wither. Trials and tribulations brought forth by sinners and temptations will challenge. That is a fact of life. However, holding true the way of the righteous shall allow me to stand firm, while the unjust blow by as leaves, and wither in their ways. As a Christian, it is my duty to try to help and save, but never at the price of my own spiritual soundness. I may catch a leaf or two, and return them to the tree. To do so would be to share the gift of enlightenment; not in the sense of knowledge to better my fellow man, but to share in the joy of knowing myself to be in the Lord's favor. While I must walk amongst both the godly and ungodly, it is my duty as a servant of the Lord to be able to adhere to His plan firmly. As a person who has both sinned and challenged the godly in the past, with grim satisfaction, I see the error in my ways. If I can grow day by day with my guides and the Lord as my armor then I can once again be considered amongst the godly, the blessed. I see the Lord's face in many facets of my life on a daily basis now. The veil of ignorance has been lifted and my blessings are as apparent as the proverbial smack in the face. The Lord is at my side, even though it took 34 years to see Him. He greeted me with open arms and blessings a-plenty, even though I had been a sinner and a blasphemer. All He has asked of me is to let Him lead me in His way. As a soldier of 14 years, I had become accustomed to taking orders from those who were appointed over me. It's hard to believe that, for all my life, I have been ignoring directions from Him Who is appointed over all. Until now.

Psalm 2

The men who pursue the illusion of power in this world have forsaken it in the next, conspiring against the just in pursuit of vanity. We need to seek the power of the Lord rather than crave others to seek our own. Vanity and material worth are hard obstacles to overcome in this life without the Lord. We are surrounded by it every day. Who has the nicer car, bigger house, larger paycheck? Who can control more subordinates, or who is subordinate to the least amount of others? I myself am guilty of vanity. I had the apartment, the girl, the car, and the ego to match. All are gone now, and I find myself nearly perfectly content. Without the Lord I would be a wreck. A little over a week ago I was sitting in the waiting room of the emergency department of a hospital, shaking, sick, feeling like walking death, due to alcohol detoxification. Waiting to be seen, I sat and watched two people, who owed me <u>NOTHING</u>, cry tears for me, because they knew I was suffering. My ego was in the bucket I was holding in case I vomited, and I realized I had something more valuable than I have ever had. I have two guardian angels sent by the Lord to keep me alive, so I can fulfill God's plan for me. Take the girl, the car, the apartment. Just leave me your angels, O Lord.

Psalm 3

At times it may seem as if the entire world is stacked up against you. Enemy after enemy, some of whom, we must remember, are our brothers, block the path. These are doubters, scoffers, and self-righteous people. Sometimes we ourselves are our own enemy. Not that we are evil or possessed, per se, but, rather, that we are lost. In my case, I know I am prone to self-destructive behavior, because it's what I've been accustomed to. Day by day, the Lord is changing that part of me. As I grow in the embrace of the Lord, there are those who continue to challenge my change, trying to draw me back into the world of disdain and loathing. Attempting to love someone in spite of their ill intentions toward you is a huge challenge. It becomes easier with practice in the way of the Lord, but it's difficult initially. Part of me wants to fight back, to lash out at those who would see me fail. But, with each passing moment, I grow closer to being at peace with not only myself, but the world around me. As I grow in this way, I not only grow closer to God, but also to my fellow brothers. The day that I embrace my enemy in kindness will be the day that I have been blessed with clarity of a divine origin.

Psalm 4

If I can lay my head on my pillow each night, knowing I walked a righteous path that day, then I am growing. I can not fear judgment from my fellows, for it is born in vanity and guided by blindness. There is only one true Judge, and there are many with their backs turned to Him. I have turned to face Him, for He has become all too familiar with my back. I was greeted with a welcoming smile, and I could feel my ailments lifting. It will take time, and I will never be perfect. However, being able to rejoice in the feeling of being lifted is a gift. Weights that are heavier than I can hardly bare are being torn to pieces as I learn of Him. In spite of all the troubles I currently face, I can still smile. Those who know of me and my situation would think I have no reason to smile. They think this, because they cannot see the Lord standing by my side. He smiles with me, and embraces me when my troubles attempt to grab hold. I'm facing many obstacles in the near future, terrifying obstacles. Be my shield, my Lord; guide me, and make me strong. Show me, Your child, that I am, indeed, a blessed child of light, and allow me to earn Your favor. Allow me to atone for the last 34 years.

Psalm 5

God will smite the wicked; not with evils or death, but simply by denying them His favour. Those who deny His presence and His kingship will not earn that which is most precious: to be able to stand with the Lord as their shield. Forsake Him, and you'll be forsaken. The path is simple. Love the Lord, and acknowledge that you are <u>NOT</u> the most powerful force in the universe. There is a Higher Power. You can't touch or grasp Him, but you can feel Him all around you at all times. I spent my entire life considering myself the only force driving my destiny. This ignorance placed too much power and responsibility in my hands. It brought me to where I am today: kneeling on the Lord's doorstep, asking for His help in rebuilding a new and better life; one where I am not considered among the forsaken and lost; one where His guidance will fill me with a goodness and purity that will one day overflow from my spirit and spill out to others. I am ashamed of how far I've come unguided, and with such disastrous results. I rejoice in knowing that, in spite of this, it is not too late. I am saved by His grace and blessed by His hand. I must not squander this incredible gift.

Psalm 6

I am weak. Self-pity plagues my fractured ego. Tears have fallen by the thousands from my eyes and soaked my shirts with vain complaints. Happiness would escape me at every corner, and I never understood why. Once again, I am weak; too frail alone to grasp joy and clutch it to myself. Without the Lord, everything happens <u>TO</u> me. With the Lord, everything happens <u>FOR</u> me. Realizing this difference shows me exactly how futile my past frets have been. It is so easy to victimize oneself, to blame others, to blame God. It is much more difficult to give credit; credit to others and to God for strengthening you. Every struggle is a journey of developing oneself. How you perceive it determines the benefits, or the costs. Where I once sat and cried for all that I had felt robbed of, I now give thanks for having received strength. Happiness was not running from me, but I was running from it, and chasing that which would ultimately bring me down; farther from content, and farther from God. I am weak, but the Lord is strong. With Him I am safe from the siren's alluring songs of self-pity and darkness. With Him, failure becomes potential, losses become lessons; and I become strong.

Psalm 7

I see now the wickedness I had within me; how I stood in the shadow of the fallen and felt at home there. I didn't know that, by simply walking a righteous path, I would be saved, and the quality of my life improved by leaps and bounds. It's disheartening to know I stood in such a bad posture before the Lord for so long. When sober, I would try to live a karmatic lifestyle of doing unto others. When drinking, I was truly wicked. I wanted to hurt and maim others, so that they could be my brethren in sorrow. I hurt those closest to me: my friends and my loved ones. Those who would try to help were met by the blade of my tongue and the wickedness I had buried within me. My own brother, whom I would call my best friend, has fallen victim to my self-righteous, vain rantings of self-pity and entitlement. Though he still loves me deeply, he must keep his distance, to protect his heart and his family. But, through the grace of God, I shall one day be back in my family's favor. As I read the Word of the Lord, and grow in His embrace, I can feel the wickedness leaving me with every breath; being drawn from me as a blade that had been cast through me my entire life, and rusted at the hilt from tears of self-inflicted anguish. Thank you, Lord, for this.

Psalm 8

The earth and all of its fruits and features are a gift from God to man, to do with as we see fit. Whether we honor this gift and God with our actions, or take for granted that which has been given us, is a choice. Even the ground beneath our feet was placed there to serve a purpose. In reading Psalm 8, I am reminded that the greatest gift and challenge that we have is free will: the freedom to follow Him, or to walk away. We have been made a little lower than the angels; yet we have the ability to turn our backs on God, or to let Him hold us to His breast. In the past, my own free will has been my undoing. With no guidance other than life's experiences, and the influence of other people, I had woven a dark quilt that I lay with each night. It is by my own free will that I now read the Word, and write my story; so that, one day, when I am truly saved, I can say that this is where it began, and where I let God guide my will instead of man and his trappings. On this path I will learn to treasure all things big and small. There is a pain in knowing all of the blessings and gifts that I have given up by my own free will; the people who loved me being the most prevalent. However, all is not lost. Through the Word, I shall once again count my blessings, and gain a higher appreciation for that which I have taken for granted for so long. And, for that, I will be truly grateful.

Psalm 9

I am but a man; and my greatest enemy dwells within me. The Lord will smite the enemy within, as long as I let Him in my heart. The impure part of my being that clings to my soul as a tumor will be cast into the pit from whence it came. I have a disease of the mind, a warped and distorted perception of purpose. When I lose sight of the Lord, I hand the controls over to the disease. Each time I find myself waking from a nightmare, I pray that it has only been a dream. Then I crawl back to the Lord's feet, full of shame and guilt, only to be met with warmth and comfort. He has not forsaken me! Even though I meet all the criteria of the heathen, I am still His son! He has a deeper plan for me. He tries to tell me this, even though, at times, it has fallen on deaf ears, and for so long. As I open my ears and my heart, I begin to see that deeper meaning to my existence. Although His plan for me is gradually being revealed, I wait in eager anticipation for His workings within me. I can feel it, day by day, hour by hour, moment to moment. My heart swells with every beat, now that I can feel His presence. Take the worst parts of myself from me, and do with them as You will. But make me pure, and use me for Your purpose.

Psalm 10

The path I have walked until this point has been the path of the fatherless. Not of my earthly father, for he has always been there; but of my heavenly Father. My actions and intentions were always those that I mistakenly thought were acceptable, because the Lord's face did not shine down on me. I was in hiding; and being there, I could do as I please. Being agnostic, the concept of last minute redemption comforted me in my unjust ways. I thought that, if the Lord does exist, maybe a death bed confession will save my soul. IF! My thought process had always been so clouded and self-righteous. I would always place my own wants and desires ahead of a just cause. My yearnings had been fed by a Fatherless existence (by choice), and I have reaped what I have sown. I would not so much call it suffering His wrath, but, rather, suffering brought on by my own distrust in any type of higher power. For so long, God did not exist to me. I carried on in my daily doings with reckless abandon, not fearing any repercussions, the least being those that were divine. I was a heathen in the flesh, a poster child of wrong decisions. Yet, He never gave up on me! I am still here, and alive! I have not been smitten; nay, I have indeed been blessed! One after another, His blessings rain down upon me each day, as a cleansing downpour that washes my soul. I can once again stand proud. Not in my own pride, but, rather, in His grace.

Psalm 11

I can rejoice in knowing now that I can trust the Lord. I can call on His name when I suffer, and praise Him when I feel joy. I had never realized exactly how alone I felt. No matter how many friends and acquaintances I had, I was lonely. The loneliness fed my addiction like a herd of gazelles is food to lions. It was plentiful and always present, and I turned to the bottle for relief. The alcohol only emblazoned my loneliness with anger, and I would try to cast it from myself with intentions of calamity. Often I succeeded. The loneliness I felt, the void inside me, was infinite. Nothing I could do could fill it. In the rooms we often talk of this infinite void. The only thing that can fill an infinite space is an infinite presence; and the only infinite presence is that of God. No bottle can possibly cure a lack of the Lord in my life. No person can sit in His stead, and accomplish what He does. I tried long and hard my entire life to find that magic solution to what was missing. People, things, and my bane: alcohol. I managed to put together a substantial amount of sober time at one point. I thought I had beaten my demons, and moved on to the next chapter in my life. After a relapse, I can now look back and say with sincerity that, during those two and a half years of sobriety, I had never felt lonelier. I was just existing. If I had then what I have now, which is acceptance of the Lord, I would have never felt lonely. Today, I can truly say that, while I may never escape loneliness completely, I will never BE alone; because He is with me.

Psalm 12

I reach out to the Lord for help now each day. Sometimes it's as simple as help getting out of bed and getting dressed. Sometimes it's for help to keep the tears from my eyes when I am reminded of things I've lost. Most of all, I ask for help in my spiritual growth. Help me, Lord, feel Your presence throughout the day, and to stand amongst the doubters, and hold my head high. I know that, in my personal life, there are three types of people who will read what I have written. The first will be the believers, who will stand with me and rejoice in hearing my voice as a son of God. The second are the agnostics. They care for me deeply and only want to see me succeed. While they may not know of the Lord, they will appreciate the fact that I have found something that inspires me to be a better person. The third are the atheists. I have many associates who simply do not believe, and I do not judge them for this. They may, however, judge me, and stand in utter disbelief of my turning to God. "Desperation", they'll think; and they'll be absolutely correct. I am desperate beyond measure to find my deeper meaning; not to just simply "be". When I limp my way through life, with no intentions other than to do myself harm in pursuit of relief, I am lost, as though I'm lost in the woods with no sense of direction. Helpless, hopeless, and just existing without direction. I have turned to God, not by force of man or the Lord Himself, but of desperation. I came to Him in despair, where I was humbled, and now sit amongst His children, and praise Him for all that He has brought forth unto me.

Psalm 13

I am alive! This alone is a miracle by God's own hand. I had felt forsaken for so long, that it had become all that I knew. The sad part is, I had felt forsaken by my fellow man, with a total disregard for the Lord. I placed value in something that was, for all intents and purposes, useless. To be in the favor of my brothers and sisters acted as a bandaid on a wound that required a tourniquet. The fact that I was standing knee deep in a world of material satisfaction was but fuel for that which ultimately brought me to my knees. I lacked any perception of a divine force; one that would drag me from my hole of hopelessness, place upon my head an helmet of serenity, arm me with a sword of righteousness to fight my demons, and clothe me in armor to repel the inevitable onslaughts of vanity. Trudging through that deep, dark swamp of godlessness for so long had twisted me, and turned me into something that I couldn't bare to look at in the mirror. I wore shame on my head and guilt across my back. As I said, I am still alive. A miracle. Not only am I alive but I have the privilege to pray each day, and to know that my voice is heard. I have the honor of knowing that, though I was once a twisted, vile creature, I now stand cleansed. I look in the mirror and I do not feel the need to look away. For I see a child of light; a man who leaves the house each day with a full heart, and an open mind ready to see all that God does in my life every day; and ready, ever so ready, to grow closer to Him.

Psalm 14

Psalm 14 is kind in using the word "fool" to describe those who have declared that there is no God. I spent my entire life as a "fool". I was raised Roman Catholic, and was forced to attend church by my father. We had made a deal that I only <u>HAD</u> to attend until my confirmation; at which point, it would become my own choice whether or not to attend. My confirmation couldn't come fast enough. I would sit through mass, and not hear a word. I would study the grain structure of the wooden bench in front of me, looking for patterns and such. I hated getting on my knees. Then I would attend catechism, and stare out the window at the trees, once again not hearing a word. Once I was confirmed, I never returned to church. I had declared God to be fictitious long before I had ever even given Him a chance. To add to the disgrace, I resented my father for forcing me to go. Now, as an adult, I understand that he was just trying to introduce me to God. I realized that, even before I found God myself. I have much guilt for having resented him for that. Growing up, I was always told that I was intelligent by my parents, friends, teachers, and, eventually, by my co-workers. I grew prideful in believing it to be my greatest trait and most powerful tool. To insult my intelligence was a way to instantly infuriate me beyond boiling. Today, as I write this, I can confess I have lived my entire life as nothing more than a "fool". Knowing mere facts, as opposed to knowing God, is as a puddle to an ocean. I was a "fool"; but He is changing that right now.

Psalm 15

Honor thy neighbor. Practice kindness until it becomes second nature, as natural as breathing. There is no room for prideful pursuits in the tabernacle of the Lord. I am guilty, and confess to the Lord, that I have taken advantage of His people. Those who struggle with addiction know that we are master manipulators. We so easily prey on the sympathy of others to acquire the means to pursue ill gains. In my addiction, my greatest victims have been my parents. In 2010, I returned from a year-long deployment to Kuwait, and was welcomed home as the family hero. My parents had put together a bedroom for me, and my mother had filled a wall with pictures of me; a shrine to her pride in her soldier son. Within a few short months my drinking had escalated to the point where I would lock myself in my room for days with my bottles, hiding from them. I knew they sat in the living room and wept for their fallen hero. My shame was so deep that I couldn't face them. At its worst, I had started to keep a small bucket under my bed to use when I needed to go to the bathroom. God forbid that I should stumble past my parents to use the toilet, and then be confronted by my father about my drinking. I couldn't face them. Ignorance was bliss. I think, in a way, it was the same for them. Even though they knew I was in my room, lost within myself, at least they knew <u>WHERE</u> I was. I put them through so much, that I don't know if I can ever fully atone. Today, I rely on the kindness of others here in my early recovery, and do my best to stay mindful of that. I am grateful beyond measure, a true sign that God is working through me and giving me clarity. Thank you, Lord.

Psalm 16

God will not let me fall into the pits of hell; whether it be the hell of this life, or the next. I call out to Him, and put Him above me; for I am but a lowly man. Father, embrace me each morning as I head out into the world amongst Your children, both the pure and impure. Strengthen me, and keep my eyes dry. Lift from my mind the swirling torturous remembrances of my wicked past. Do not let me forget my wrongs, for they teach me of Your rights. Keep me at peace with all things in life, so that, in death, I can become an angel of Your court. I will hold You high as You hold a firm hand in between me, and the way of the fallen. Please, God, guide me each and every day, and remove from me my love for escape; for escape is just an illusion, a temporary change in my state of mind that kills me ever so quietly, and robs me of the joys of being present and in the moment. It weighs down my soul with chains of iniquity. Do not allow me to hide from You. Cast Your light upon me when I try to darken my world. I cannot trust myself to care for my soul and life; for I have done nothing but forsake both in the past. It is only with You, and through Your grace, that I have been saved. Even the deepest, darkest parts of myself cower in fear in Your presence. I smile and revel in that feeling. It's almost as if I'm weightless, and set free from bondage. Even now, as I write in praise of You, I smile, because I can feel Your work being done within my soul.

Psalm 17

To think that the Lord hears <u>MY</u> words each day, in my prayers, is so comforting. To be able to talk to Him now, after spending so long ignoring Him, is humbling; a true lesson in forgiveness. He whose tenets I have broken and spat on looks to me now and speaks with me as His child. You just need to simply ask for forgiveness with an honest heart, and He enters your life with the force of an avalanche. Admit your wrongs. Admit you are powerless over His realm. In recovery, our first step is to admit that we are powerless over our substance of choice, and that our lives have become unmanageable. I am powerless over alcohol, and so much more. He is all-powerful. Even sober, my life was unmanageable, because I had no guidance. I was simply "just not drinking". I had no joy, no reason to feel uplifted, other than the fact that I was sober that day. Don't misunderstand me: being sober and miserable in recovery is always better than being intoxicated and content. However, finding something in recovery that keeps you going and growing is the key to maintaining your happiness. For me, that has become God. My only regret is that it took me so long to realize He was there, waiting for me. All that is within me, that has plagued my story with horrifying tales of destruction, is being changed by His will alone, not mine. Let Your will be mine, O Lord. Guide me, so that I may walk with You, rather than against You.

Psalm 18

The Lord shall deliver me from my enemies. With a force I have never before known, He shall enter my life and sweep me up into His mercy. Those who stand against me in my path of righteousness shall be smitten by Him, and removed from my journey. In reading Psalm 18, I am reminded that I am my own worst enemy. I have brought upon myself all of the evils that have tainted my journey thus far. A godless existence had left me naked in the cold and bitter realities of this world. I have struggled to endure, but have always found myself back in the same situations. As an alcoholic, I am prone to insanity. We in recovery know the definition of insanity: to repeat the same actions, and expect different results. I was continuing to live a lifestyle of ill proportions, and simply waited for things to right themselves. If only I had asked for Him sooner, I would have ended the insanity spiral. However, now that I stand in awe of His power, I cannot look back. I cannot be mournful of my past, for it was wrought with darkness. I shall not mourn that which brought me down. My enemy, alcohol, shall not bear the honor of my mourning. Nay, God cast it from me with a furious rage; for I am His son, and He wishes me well. He wants to see me succeed, for He has a plan for me. I have a purpose in this plan, and I shall NOT be smitten by mine enemy!

Psalm 19

Redemption. I thought it was lost by the error in me, and that one such as myself could never be redeemed; both in the eyes of my earthly brethren, and in those of a Lord I did not fully know. As I sing His praise now, and read His Word, I am relieved of the stain I had on my heart. It was a feeling of worthlessness. I could see in my day to day life that my fellows would look down on me in judgment and pity, seeing me as broken and lost, as if set in a boat and pushed from the shore, and growing smaller and smaller as I drifted off. I thought for sure that if my fellow man saw me in this fashion, then, surely, so did the Lord. By placing value in the judgment of man, 1 blinded myself to what really mattered. HIS opinion of me is all that really matters; for His opinion is perfect. Watching myself be saved, being drawn back to shore, and again growing, has changed my perception. Let those that would doubt me cast their stones of judgment. Let them tempt me with their ways. Let them dig their holes, and, once done, and too deep to crawl out of, let them see my outstretched hand. Redemption is simply an outstretched hand to the Lord, and to His children sent to guide you to Him. One day, I shall have the joy of helping another seek redemption, and to share in my joy. As for now, I follow the Lord, and I follow my guides. For I have lived without purpose, until He took my hand.

Psalm 20

The fact that I am alive, and that I wake each day, grateful and with a smile, is proof that I am one of the Lord's anointed. I praise His name, and keep one eye to the heavens, as I keep the other on my path. I shall not veer off course, for I have been blessed with the knowledge of Him, Who is greater than all. Most importantly, He's greater than me. By willingly giving to Him my free will, I have not lost it. I still have the ability to decide and to make choices as I please. However, now the arrows of my actions are guided true. My quiver is blessed, and my bolts no longer tainted. Hell can try to take me, but it can't hold me, if my heart is true. The pits are not my home, and the vile are not my brethren. Recovery and its messengers tell us that it's necessary to change people, places and things in our lives in order to change our lifestyle and prevent relapse. This is very true. As the Psalms say in many ways that those who dwell among the ill shall stay ill. Those who sit in unholy places shall dwell there. Those who crave the power and gold will reap nothing in the end. In my case, allowing the Lord into my life has alleviated all of those things. He has sent me NEW people. Many of them had been there all along, but I had not realized it, until I was in distress. He gave me new places. Holy, untainted places. He gave me new things; things that I never had before: like faith, a Bible, and the desire to interpret His Word to save my soul.

Psalm 21

The righteous may ask of the Lord, and they shall receive; for the righteous ask for good things. Those with clean and sober souls shall reap the rewards of faith; just as those with clean and sober bodies shall reap the rewards of sobriety. I have learned that, while having a body that is free of poisons leads to a better existence, having a soul that is free of toxins leads to a more pure existence. Toxins, like greed, envy, and lust, are to the soul as alcohol is to the body. They taint our path with ill decisions, and draw us farther from the Lord. I had never been farther from the Lord than when I was content in my sins. I had carried nearly every sin on my shoulders as if they were a thorny pauldron. It was invisible to my fellow sinners, but blatantly obvious to those who sat in God's shadow and grace. As I toss my tainted armor to the wayside, and ask the Lord to please forgive and guide me, I am cleansed. There is salvation in humbling yourself before the Lord, and giving Him all of yourself by choice, as He has given you all of yourself by His will. I praise him each day for accepting my offering of myself to Him. Burnt, used, and abused, He accepts the return of my life and will, and He shall repair it; for He is perfect.

Psalm 22

To this point, no Psalm has spoken to me in the way that Psalm 22 has. Even as an agnostic, I would cry out to the heavens: "God, why have You forsaken me?" All that is wrought in my life, all that is twisted and torn, it must be by divine leverage that all of this has been brought upon my head. I was blaming God for my sorrows. In active addiction, blame is our blanket. It keeps us warm, and protects us from the truth. I had no room for faith when my life was going well. I could not share credit, for it was the food for my ego, and I couldn't let it go hungry. God seemed real only when I felt I was being forsaken. This backward thinking robbed me of His presence. I stole the Lord's glory, and held it high as my own. As I walk forward in life now, eyes open to all of His workings in it, I have remorse for my actions of the past. I was wrong, and I own my faults today because He allows me to, with a clean heart. Perfection is a state of being that is reserved solely for the Lord. Though I will never reach it myself, I can grow closer. In my faith, as well as in my recovery, I <u>WILL</u> own all of my iniquities, for they are but mine. God has allowed these imperfections within me, so that I may learn from them, share my experiences, and help others. I am but a wrench; a tool to be used when needed, to accomplish a task. For He has many tasks, and I am his sturdy wrench.

Psalm 23

I have indeed walked through the valley of the shadow of death, as have many of my brethren. The path is strewn with the bodies of the fallen, and those who have forsaken the anointing of the Lord. This is the only path down which the pursuit of ill fruit shall lead you. Alcoholism was killing me, both physically and spiritually. I strolled the valley daily, in both fear and delight; for alcohol is a cunning mistress. Absent from the audience of the Lord, I wandered the barren fields of decay, dying beneath my skin more and more with each step. Sick with the disease of faithlessness, the sun had not shone in my world, for it feared my loathing of it. It wasn't until I was among the strewn, fallen and forsaken that the sun did rise; pulled into the sky by the will of the Lord; for He wanted me to see it. I was not meant to be just an ornament, a decoration in the fields of darkness. Purpose fell on and into me, and I arose to navigate the fields guided by the sun and His glory. At the edge of the pit lay the mountain of faith, and the handholds of the humbled. As I have begun my climb, and watched the pit grow smaller beneath me, it becomes harder to look down. For what I left down there . . . is terrifying . . .

Psalm 24

The gates of salvation await my arrival. When my purpose has been fulfilled in this world, I shall behold them in all their glory. I will sit upon the mountain with the just, and join them in singing praise to Him. A scenario, as a fairy tale to the lost, is but truth to the saved; much as it is in recovery. In early recovery, we listen to those who have been saved from their addictions. They speak of their beautiful lives full of joy and prosperity. It seems like such a fairy tale, and so far out of reach. Reeling in shock from the stark realities of sobriety, we struggle with hope, and faith in ourselves, to do the next right thing. With faith in the Lord, I trust Him to guide me to the next right thing. The only faith I need in myself is to stay faithful to the Lord. If I keep Him as my Guardian, then I can trust that my path is true. All it takes is simple faith, humbleness, and being open to His will. I receive His blessings at every turn, because I have learned that He is there! Every day I see in my actions and choices that He is doing His work. There is none who could convince me otherwise; for He has taken hold, and told me that I have value. He has told me that I may not behold His gates, until my purpose has been fulfilled in His name. I have a job to do, and it's the best job I will ever have.

Psalm 25

Trust has always been a challenge in my journey. As one of the afflicted, I am prone to iniquities. To be able to finally have someone to trust fully is heart-wrenching; not out of sorrow, but, instead, of joy. I can trust the Lord, for He is perfect. He steals not from my plate nor my pocket; nay, He fills both. He does not lie to me, nor hide His intentions, and He holds no secret agendas. I am not His hobby or side project, but I am His son. He loves me and cares for me as a Father ought. He lifts my ailments through His Word, and brings me to stand in a just posture. This is what having a Higher Power is all about: being humbled, and seeking to be trustworthy, as your actions reflect the influence of your Higher Power. Earning the trust of those who I have wronged in the past is part of the journey that God has placed me on. I know I will never regain the trust of some, for the Lord has determined that it is not necessary. My wrongs were many and deep; too deep for some to recover. I accept this, as I accept and TRUST the wisdom of the Lord. Everything that is to come is but of His design, and it's perfect. I stand afflicted, yet strong; for He bolsters my being and drives my thirst for salvation.

Psalm 26

Deliverance. Deliver me from all of mine enemies, and allow me to congregate amongst the pure of heart. Let a sinner be saved, as I walk a path I have not known; that of one with a full heart, and an empty mind, and ready to receive His Word, and His guidance. Deliver me from myself, so that I may know that I am not the only voice in this world. Let Yours fill my mind, and take from me my thoughts of imperfection. For Your voice is perfect, its callings true, its directions just. I have suffered in the struggle of my self-inflicted absence of God; trying to rationalize all that is, solely through the power of my own feeble human mind. That's the same mind that became stricken with a disease that, for all intents and purposes, steals my will and turns it toward self-destruction. Veiled under the guise of a friend who wants to simply steal away my pain, this disease secretly waits to kill me, to take from me that which God has given me, and to cast me into the pits from whence it was birthed. Deliver me, O Lord, from mine enemy. In Jesus' name I pray that You stay this disease, turn it to stone, and let it not progress. Let it not block my journey from the darkness into the light; for, by Your grace, things shall change, and I will once again have value in my purpose. Slay my demons, my God, for Your child is assailed, but not broken.

Psalm 27

As I experience life anew in having God with me, I have come to some realizations. You do not have to perish to be able to dwell in the presence of the Lord. He is with me now, just as He has always been. The blinded has been touched, and made to see. I now see His tabernacle, and know that I am invited inside, where I can sit in comfort, knowing I am of Him. He shall protect me from all that is sent against me, for the walls of His tabernacle are ever so strong. Psalm 27:10 says: "When my father and my mother forsake me, then the Lord will take me up". I know my parents have not forsaken me; nay, they love me deeper than I know. At times, I was under the illusion that I was forsaken by them. When my father cast me from his home, I saw it as being tossed to the dogs, as if I was worthless. Today, in clarity, I see that I was not discarded, nor unloved. I was cast out because he could no longer bear the anguish I brought into his home; to sit and watch his child die slowly, slipping farther each day, and knowing there was nothing that could be done. I can't imagine the deepness of that sorrow. I hope and pray that now, as I dwell in the house of the Lord, my parents can take solace in my safety; for He protects me.

Psalm 28

In the Lord's hands I have placed my will, lest I be led by the wicked into the pit. For the wicked, both within and without me have a silver tongue that beckons under the guise of friendship, conspiring against me with the promise of false prosperity. The Lord, in His infinite wisdom and His endless mercy, has opened my eyes to the hidden agendas of these things. I know to steer away from them, for they will be struck down by Him when the time is come. Whilst the Lord will not remove every last challenge I will face, He <u>WILL</u> bolster my spirit, so that I may overcome. Living within His kinship, feeling His Holy Spirit, grants me the power to move about in my days without reckless abandon; my choices true, my actions correct, my persistence steady. I go forward on the steed of faith I have been given, for He has places that I need to go, people I need to touch, and possibly even souls to save. To think of where I am going in relation to where I have been is almost unfathomable; so I simply do not attempt to. It is not my place to understand, but, rather, to just trust in Him, and experience the journey. A force I have never known until now pushes my change from within me. I can see it, I can feel it, and for the first time, I can honestly say, I am excited, for the spiritual path I am on in life. No longer a void, it is filled with hope and joy!

Psalm 29

The Lord has blessed me with peace. He has given me soundness of mind, so that I may undo the calamity that had become of His child. Man is but man, but the Lord is above all. I am but a simple man, who tried to control the world around me. How humorous it must have been for Him to watch as I tried to be so powerful. Powerlessness is the first lesson in recovery. Having been in recovery, I accepted that I was powerless over alcohol, until I relapsed. I had never fully accepted that I was powerless over the world around me. I could not see that it was HIM behind the controls, rather than myself. I tried to bear the load of the divine, and failed miserably. It's humorous to me now, in spite of the consequences. To simply let go would have saved me sooner; but I mourn not my past, for He has brought me forth, and lifted me when the time was right. He had this plan long before I ever picked up that first drink. Every experience I've had is a lesson to fertilize my being, and to make me into what He has deemed me to be. God willing, my learnings will turn into lessons for others, so that I may smite the suffering of another, in His name.

Psalm 30

Strength in recovery is hard to acquire. It takes time and support before we truly become strong. All the while, we must remember that we will never be stronger than our demons (substance); for, when we believe so, we open the doors and allow it in, believing ourselves to be strong enough to control it. To gain strength through admitting weakness seems like an oxymoron. However, in my new-found faith, I have found this to be one of the biggest blessings. By admitting to God that I am weak, He takes me unto Himself, and grants me strength. I have never had the privilege of knowing His force driving my life. I had forsaken that through my choices and lack of faith. As I stand now, and accept how frail I truly am, I am filled with strength. God will never make me more powerful than alcohol, though He could. I was not meant to be more powerful than my enemy. Nay: instead, I was meant to stand against my enemy in my frailty, as an example that even the meek can conquer the mighty with the Lord behind them. My foe is strong and alluring. Though I sat with him, and we communed together for so long, I must now turn away. He shall not bear the privilege of taking this world from me; for, though I be weak, My Savior is strong. He looks at you, and scoffs at your illusion of power, for it is born in the pit from whence He casts things, to be discarded.

Psalm 31

Shame. Before the Lord entered into my life through faith, my cup had overflowed with shame. Through the will of the Lord on this day, and in those to come, my shame is being transformed into courage. Shame is but a resentment towards ourselves; and, in recovery, we learn that resentments are the number one offender, the leading cause of relapses. We are trained by our fellowship and sponsors to let go of resentments, both toward ourselves, and toward others. My training was deep and well thought out, but it was not perfect. The shame never left me, and my inward resentments lingered. Through God, I am slowly cleansing the shame from my being. With every righteous action, I grow cleaner inside. I am not ashamed to admit that I have traveled to the Lord's doorstep, seeking His wisdom. There are plenty of people in my life who will pass their judgments on this, and they will be met kindly by my courage. I had not known relief from my self-loathing, until He came. The freedom from regrets is so soothing to the spirit, that it makes my soul blossom as a flower in the garden amongst weeds. As I heal day by day, my regrets are replaced by gratitude for the chance to experience shame and to have it lifted, and to behold the pit before entering his tabernacle. For now, I can share this with others and provide warnings. I can claim knowledge: that to be righteous in His name is to be truly saved from a dastardly existence!

Psalm 32

As a sinner, I have brought forth into my world anguish piled ever so high on my back. I would call out, only to have it fall on deaf ears, because my callings were selfish and unjust. I would pray to keep my bottle full, to fill my wallet and to smite those which I had passed judgment on. I would ask to have my life blessed with vanity and carnal sins. What type of God did I think I was speaking to? I didn't even believe in Him, anyway, so, from whence did this insanity come? Today I pray for just causes. I pray for guidance and strength in my faith. I pray for others who ail, so that they may be alleviated. I pray in thanks for Gods workers who toil so diligently in my life to keep me true. I pray just to say thank You. Let it be known that I am grateful for the privilege of knowing that, once again, I am on a righteous walk. Let it be known that I give all of myself to Thee, to do with in Your workings. The wrath of the Lord will be mighty upon the sinners and heathen, but it shall not fall on my head; for I am on the Lord's payroll. Each morning, my eyes open, and I clock in, ready for the day's work. I shall wear the hat of the day. There are many hats on the rack which I must choose from each day; but I shall watch the one of sin become covered with dust, for it shall not feel the warmth of my head evermore.

Psalm 33

With the Lord by my side, I shall not stand in the counsel of the wicked. By mouth of man or slight of my disease, I shall not take ear. Purity lies solely within His teachings and within His words. Let my mouth move to speak His doings, so that I may be but a messenger to my brothers. My life I give unto Him, for I have abused it and neglected it myself. I stood at a crossroads, sick and disgusted with what I had become. As Psalm 33:19 says, "To deliver their soul from death, and to keep them alive in famine", I was dying, and my soul starving. Today, I am not dead, and my soul's belly is full. He has given unto me a <u>NEW</u> life; one in which I will not live in the shadow of my self-inflicted abuse, one in which His Word guides me to each destination. For He has taken me, the spiritually bankrupt, and given me hope. Life begins anew with a new found sense of belonging. Death has left my dwelling, and I no longer fear his scythe. The power of the Lord is too much for him to bear. He is my protector. He stays that which would try to take my life, and performs His miracles from within. My mind, though diseased, no longer ails.

Psalm 34

The Son of God suffered for us. He is the most righteous amongst us. A common trend I am noticing in the Psalms is that the righteous have endured suffering. Psalm 34:19 says: "Many are the afflictions of the righteous: but the Lord delivereth him out of them all". As we suffer we grow. Whether we grow spiritually, or grow vainly, is solely determined by our own perceptions. Do we perceive our tribulations as teachings, or as punishments? Do we shrink down in our seats, and turn away as a beaten dog, or do we sit upright, and ask for guidance? I now see purpose in the sufferings I have endured; for they were but the stepping stones that I needed to reach a higher plane of understanding. My self-pity and ignorance have been replaced, once again, by gratitude. I am who I am today because of my experiences on my path. These have given me the tools to use, rather than the wounds to lick. Accepting the past, and moving forward in spite of it, is critical to recovery. Wallow not in the pools of the disheartened; for it is a tempting trap in the beginning. Instead, bask in the glory of the Power that delivereth; for He alone can. I have tried by my own hand, but a temporary stay of the beast was all I accomplished. I don't see the beast now. He hides from the presence of the Lord.

Psalm 35

Those that would rejoice in my failure shall be kept at bay by the will of the Lord. There are those who look at me now, and I can see it in their eyes. They wonder in disbelief why, even after all my misdoings, I am still blessed. They wonder how I still have employment, how I'm not in jail, how I'm not dead. These things are gifts from the Lord. For, though I was a sinner, He saw the desire within me; the desire that He now nurtures with his grace. He has called unto me, and given me purpose. He has told me that it is time for my suffering to end, and that I am finally ready to do His work. He has left me that which I need to carry on, and taken those things that would hold me back. He has removed people from my life who would bring me down, and He has taken objects that fed my vanity. He has replaced my ill gains and my void, and He has filled me with Himself. He has given me angels, under the guise of simple persons, for me to commune with. All of these gifts grant me the foundation upon which to build my salvation. For by my hands His will shall be done. By my mouth His messages shall be delivered. By His wisdom I shall behold my salvation.

Psalm 36

Blinded to God, I feared Him not. I made my wicked bed, and lay in it every night. Ego plagued my spirit, so that I could not know my wrongdoings. Psalm 36:2 says: "For he flattereth himself in his own eyes, until his iniquity be found to be hateful". I was such a powerful force in my own life that I was shocked when I couldn't part the seas! I had absolute control, and nothing would take that from me. Oh, how so humbling, trying to think that, as I lay in a hospital bed with tubes in my veins. My delusion of power had corrupted my spirit, and left me maimed and broken. Fear gripped me at the thought of losing control over my realm. MY realm?! Did I create the land and the seas?! Did I raise the mountains up, and bring fruit to the trees?! What exactly had I done, other than sin, and complain when I did not get my way? I brought pain and suffering to others, and continued to trek forward through the guilt and shame. It was such a horrid way to live! The toxins removed from my body, both physical and spiritual, have blown the blinders from my face. My vision is full, and I see Him everywhere! The land, the seas, the mountains, and the fruit; all are by His will. My life, in the beginning, and until the end, are by His will. Praise Him, for He is good!

Psalm 37

Judgment is a right reserved for the Lord. I shall not judge others, for that is not my purpose. Instead, I must embrace all with kindness, and offer His Word to those who need it. The truly wicked will be forsaken because of their own doings; and God will protect me from them. I am truly blessed that I can no longer count myself amongst the lost. I could not help anyone with a drink in my hand, least of all myself. I could only meddle in iniquity. With the drink now absent from my life, the Lord speaks to me. I am no judge, for my wisdom does not penetrate deep enough into righteousness. I am simple, just the way He made me. When He speaks to me, it is as a feeling, not in words. Though words flow through me even now, it is the result of feelings that He has placed inside me. These feelings are still new to me; and, oh, how I revel in their joyous sweetness. Sweet as honey to the tongue are His influences to my soul. It amazes me that I've spent my life running towards affliction, only to do an about face, and discover happiness in the other. It's so simple that I can't believe I didn't realize this sooner. But, it is part of His plan, and His plan is perfect.

Psalm 38

Coming to the Lord from where I had been has been a humbling experience. Full of iniquities and covered in scars, I had wept for myself for the last time. It was time to escape the snares of self-pity and entitlement. Feeling as though I had been cast aside by the world, I had to find my rightful place among men. The mistake I made was, instead of looking to men to guide me to that place, I should have been looking to God. Psalm 38:11 says: "My lovers and my friends stand aloof from my sore; and my kinsmen stand afar off". Even those who had yet to discover the Lord could see I was ill. They lay suggestions one upon another, and offered help. Some scolded, and tried the tough love. Some embraced me, and tried the all-too-enabling pity approach, feeding into my ego of self-righteousness. I am grateful for their attempts, as their intentions were pure. However, it wasn't until I entered the house of the Lord that I truly understood a purpose that toppled my demon. Alcohol is as cunning, baffling, and powerful a foe as any man. Today, as I stand where He has placed me, and as He speaks to me, He has taken the power from my enemy.

Psalm 39

I had been dumb in my transgressions, until the Lord took me in. Not dumb, as in lacking knowledge; but, rather, as in being silent. I did not speak His Word, I did not praise Him, nor did I acknowledge His presence. I did not pray, with the exception of my cries for vain desires. My mouth did not move under His guidance. The words that fell from me were born from within, and birthed of iniquity. I praise Him; for, though so much error had encompassed my tongue, He has now taken me under His wing, and guides my words true. He speaks to me in my times of sorrow, and when I'm ailing. When I am assaulted, He stays my tongue, and fills my mind with His Word. As my lips move, and my breath leaves me in the form of words, the Lord has reins on them, as if a steed in front of his chariot. I will no longer taste the sugary sweetness of sin, though my enemy has sweetened it deep. God willing, never again shall my words be used to hurt or maim, to undermine or destroy. They shall carry Him to others, and testify that my heart is true. They shall not fall on deaf ears, for He has placed them there for His purpose!

Psalm 40

Oh, how He works and speaks to me in my time of need! When you seek His guidance, He <u>DOES</u> deliver, if your heart is true. He speaks of my story, for I am His child. Psalm 40:2 says: "He brought me up also out of an horrible pit, out of the miry clay, and set my feet upon a rock, and established my goings". My Lord, I could not have worded it better. He eases me with the trueness in which He speaks. He delivers to me the messages and the teachings that He deems I need to hear, when the time is right, and just in time to stand firm in my faith, as I push forward till redemption. Psalm 40:6 says: "Sacrifice and offering thou didst not desire; mine ears hast thou opened: burnt offering and sin offering hast thou not required". Simply accepting Him, and opening my heart to His guidance, has allowed me to hear His voice. Even now He works through me fast and with purpose. I am forgiven of my flaws, for I acknowledge and own them. He removes from me the things which He did not place there. He purifies my soul and mind through His Word with a force that I can only describe as God Himself granting me the hunger for the Word.

Psalm 41

Psalm 41:1 says: "Blessed is he that considereth the poor: the Lord will deliver him in time of trouble". In recovery, the poor are those who are still sick and suffering. "You can only keep it by giving it away" is a phrase we often hear. Giving someone the gift of recovery is to give of yourself, to do the work of the righteous. God has asked me, nay, <u>TOLD</u> me, to do His work; for there are so many that still do suffer so. Coming from that same place, and having been wrenched free from its grasp by God, He now trains me. He strengthens me, so that I may one day return there, cleansed to do His bidding: to gather my brothers, and lead them away from the suffering. Even if I must carry them one by one to the Lord, it is <u>HIS</u> will, and it must be done. Frail and feeble, because I am just a man, but as a vessel of the Lord, may others be touched by His hand through my doings. May the sick be alleviated by my words of hope and praise. May the wicked be driven off as they witness God working through me. May I ever be in His favor as I do His work. Lord, I pray that, one day, You shall look upon me, Your son, and feel satisfied that I have served Your purpose. When my mission is done, may I enter Your house, and have the light of Your presence shine upon me!

Psalm 42

As I wallowed in my agnosticism my whole life, I found myself among the doubters who tormented the faithful. "Where is your God now"? If I did not say it aloud, I most definitely thought it whenever I saw one of the faithful suffering, since it only served to validate my own misconceptions of God. So easy it is to doubt, when you have afflicted yourself with blindness. So much of the workings in this world cannot be explained; but I could explain away God, though I had never seen Him. Now, as I stand on the opposite side of the wall of self-righteousness, I atone for my misgivings. More than a simple misunderstanding, I had consciously decided to ignore God. I can't simply say "oops" and drive on in His grace. He has work for me: weeds to pull, gutters to clean. I am under His employ, and His work is just; for they are His directions handed down in love for His people. I have accepted that I have a purpose that I was not meant to fully understand. Letting go, and letting the Lord take over, without fully knowing His plan for me, fills me with joy; for it shows me, for the first time, that I have been blessed with faith.

Psalm 43

The walk of the just through this world will present us with many enemies to our Lord's cause. In recovery, it may be old acquaintances. Even though we had loved them and called them friends, we may need to look again at these relationships. If someone leads a lifestyle that may be hazardous to our faith and/or recovery, we may need to stay away. It is possible to remove someone from our life without actually forsaking them. To protect our physical health, and, more importantly, our spiritual health, is our duty as a servant of the Lord. I was trained in the army that, if you get hit with gas, put <u>YOUR</u> mask on first, <u>THEN</u> help those who may not be able to put their own on. If you go down trying to help another, then you become unable to help others. It's the same in faith and in recovery. You may want to help someone; but if it jeopardizes your own faith or recovery, then step away. Maybe the time isn't right; you may not be strong enough yet; maybe the person isn't ready to be saved. No matter what, protecting your own spiritual soundness is not selfish; it is your duty, for it is God's gift. He shall dictate when you will act through His loving guidance. When in doubt, or unsure, pray.

Psalm 44

On our journey into sobriety and, ultimately, into the good graces of the Lord, we must be wary. There are those that would lead us astray. For many of us, it is that "monkey on our back", as we like to call it. Psalm 44:15 says: "My confusion is continually before me, and the shame of my face hath covered me". Shame is a powerful state of being. It can drive us up and out in an attempt to escape, or force us to stay locked in and hidden. Shame can drive us back to our substance, for that substance offers escape from our woes; but we know it to be ever so temporary and costly. Confusion, especially in early recovery, runs rampant. "What do I do with myself? All this free time? How do I find happiness without alcohol or drugs?" We have trained our bodies and minds to believe that being sober is boring and painful. Even after a couple years sober I had found myself thinking how great it would be if I could just have a drink, and how it would alleviate my boredom. As God speaks to and through me now, all that I once used alcohol to alleviate ails me not. I am not bored. I'm not in pain. My time is full. He has given to me the tools to make alcohol obsolete.

Psalm 45

Psalm 45 speaks to me about something that I have always struggled with: love. Romantic love, not my love for alcohol; even though, at times, that is a romance in and of itself. I've had relationships in the past, but not all of the women I have courted have walked a righteous path. Romantic relationships have been the number two offender in my recovery, second only to boredom. Crimes (as I perceived them) against my heart drove me back into active addiction more times than I care to admit. My appetite for physical affection was insatiable, as I had used it to try and fill that void inside; and I had turned to all the wrong places. I am to blame for all of my failures in my love life. God removed the lust from me. Now content, I can see how broken I was. How could I possibly offer a woman anything in a relationship while living a godless existence? How could I appreciate a woman and treat her right? How could I spot one of God's daughters amongst the plethora of the lost? How blinded I was, as if searching for a sword to heal, and a bandage to maim. If God deems it so, He shall one day introduce me to one of His daughters, and her to His son. For I love the Lord, and He shall provide.

Psalm 46

The Lord is my refuge, for His house shall not be moved. The wicked will perish, and all the armies of man may not stand against Him. This is powerful; for imagining such strength is baffling. I tried to find this strength amongst my brothers and without God. I had acquired the illusion that I had found it, but it had carried me only so far. As I lay once again, broken and finally calling out to Him, He was there. He has shown me that, though I was living sober before, I had embarked on my journey in a carriage that had been missing a wheel. It would only get me up to the point where it would finally fall apart, leaving me stranded once again, lost and confused. Today, through His Word and works within me, I ride on a sturdy vessel, a holy vessel that is to carry me far beyond where I have been, or ever intended to go. His strength is so vast that it strengthens my perseverance, and motivates me by awe. Simply just experiencing the changes within me in such a short time have humbled me in meekness. So strong is my God. So weak are my foes. So glorious my journey shall be; for it is His will.

Psalm 47

Give praise to God. Give thanks to the Lord. Wake each day with gratefulness in your heart, and count your blessings. As an alcoholic in recovery, I always found it therapeutic to try to be grateful, even if for just one small thing a day. Our disease makes us prone to dwell on the negative, for that is where it lies, and does its work, weakening our spirit, so that it may once again take hold. It seeks to poison our minds with feelings of lowliness amongst our fellows, and to make us feel judged, and less than others, because we are afflicted. That is where the disease seeks to take us. My God has removed that place from my soul. It no longer exists, and my disease reels in panic; for it has no place to drag me. I love my God; and that love has brought me peace. He has sucked the wind out from under the wings of my affliction, and it plummets, helpless, for the first time since its birth. So powerful were my demons; yet, God has made them powerless by His pure will alone. I will be mindful that I will always ail, but I will be grateful that I DO NOT suffer, because He has made it so. I will praise Him, and carry His Word, so that my fellows may experience relief as I have, and rejoice.

Psalm 48

To think that I had forsaken the Lord's temple my entire life! I had no desire to see it, and even less to set foot inside. I had even playfully toyed with the idea that, if there was, in fact, a heaven and hell, and thinking that I would surely go to hell, what would I say when I got there? How would I trick the devil into taking me into his favor, to spare me an eternity of torture? How foolish! Who did I think I was? How dare I revel in thinking that I had such a talent for wickedness. Those who struggle with addiction know, just as I do, that we consider ourselves master manipulators. And I, in my infinite ego, would fantasize about tricking the first of the fallen. Oh, how far I have come. By His grace alone, I now see truth. Trickery is no longer a tool in my tool box, nor do I place any value in it. Righteousness requires no trickery. The Lord's temple echoes with truth and praises. The cleansing Light that shines in through the pillars removes the lies from my being and from my lips. As I do His bidding, I gain solace in knowing that I will never have to commune with the first of the fallen.

Psalm 49

We, who suffer, place altogether too much value on our earthly possessions. Many of us have lost them all in pursuit of satisfying our addictions. Then we make the mistake of measuring the success of our recovery by the things we manage to again acquire. I know that I behaved in just this way during my first real attempt at recovery. Psalm 49:17 says: "For when he dieth he shall carry nothing away; his glory shall not descend after him". Right now, at this very point in time, I have just what I need to survive, and to do God's bidding. It is all I need; and, if God deems that I shall not have more than this, then that is His will. I have a warm bed, food to fill my belly, a Bible, and the means to communicate to others what the Lord has asked me to. Be grateful, as I am, for all that you have. Be even <u>MORE</u> grateful for all that we have lost, for it teaches us, and grants us a deeper understanding of what is valuable, and what is birthed in vanity. Let it humble me, Lord, so that my meekness will be filled, not with wants, but with gratuity. I shall want not, for I have the Lord; therefore, I have everything I need.

Psalm 50

We have but one life in which to prove ourselves to the Lord. He has given us one chance to decide our own fates through our choices and actions; to acknowledge His Word and His way, and to follow them diligently. Recovering from addiction requires us to follow certain "rules" in just the same manner. Just don't drink or drug. Don't substitute one drug for another. Go to meetings. Get a sponsor. Go to treatment. Don't isolate. Take your medication. As self-proclaimed masters of our own destiny, we despise authority and directions. Psalm 50:17 says: "Seeing thou hatest instruction, and casteth my words behind thee". A great many of us have relapsed, because we can't follow simple instructions. We rebel against authority for no good reason. We scoff at the elders in the rooms, when they tell us "Don't date in the first year of recovery". "WHAT!? You may have 20 years sober, kind sir, but you most certainly speak nonsense!" Ahh, how foolish we are. We barely escape destroying ourselves; but, lo and behold, we are right back to trying to master our futures! Let go. Let GOD. Listen to your guides, whomever they be; and, as long as they are righteous, heed their word. For God's sake let go, and find your purpose! It most certainly cannot be at the bottom of a bottle. I already checked.

Psalm 51

Humbleness and honesty are two tenets of both the righteous, and of those in recovery. We must not only admit our wrongs, but we must own them. To accept that we are flawed is to grow closer to God, as well as to cleanse ourselves of any delusions of grandeur that would ultimately lead us back to relapse, and farther from the Lord. The Psalms sing praise to the meek, for they will inherit the earth. As recovering addicts and alcoholics, we must lower ourselves. We must understand, and accept, how truly weak we are, in both mind and spirit. When we do so, we allow both God, and our brothers and sisters in recovery, to strengthen our mind and spirit. I have learned to shut my mouth, and to open my ears, to quiet my mind, and to open my heart. The Lord fills me with hope and strength, and my fellows, who are afflicted and struggle as I do, join me in my journey en masse. We are the frail, the poor, the ailing, the broken. But we do not suffer. We can lean on each other. We can bask in the glory of the Lord, for He protects and favors the meek. We have been made to be this way, not out of spite, but out of love. Though the forsaken are the ones who wallow in vain successes, and have never known a struggle such as ours, our struggle has a purpose that is part of a grand design by which we are saved.

Psalm 52

The mouth and the tongue are powerful tools. They can be used for both good and evil purposes, to deliver messages of hope and faith, or to be used to try to topple the righteous. I had used God's gift of my own words with ill intent on a daily basis. I was blessed with an above average vocabulary, and talent for a quick assembly of snappy responses (or so I've been told). Psalm 52:4 says: "Thou lovest all devouring words, O thou deceitful tongue". Devouring words. To me, this speaks of words that are meant to devour the spirit of another. "Low blows" come to mind. I am guilty, and own that I was a champion of the devouring word. I would say things with the perfectly flawed intent of breaking someone's spirit. I would flat out LIE to accomplish my tainted goals. I was a liar. I bathed in it daily. I WAS a liar. The Lord has shown me that even the lies that I had thought would be beneficial to my recovery were still lowly lies. I had lied to my co-workers, to my friends, and to those I loved. I did not tell them I was an alcoholic. I just simply said that I didn't drink, fearing their judgment. I had to come up with lie after lie to cover my affliction. Now, by bringing my disease into the light for all to see, God has shown me that my thinking was wrong. There are so many supporters that I had no idea were waiting; ones who could have helped me, if I had been honest sooner. I am truly loved by my fellows, for they care and take pleasure in seeing me healthy. The Lord has shown me these things. Let not one more lie slip between my lips, my Lord; for my mouth now has just cause.

Psalm 53

Right from the beginning, Psalm 53:1 says: "The fool hath said in his heart, there is no God. Corrupt are they, and have done abominable iniquity: there is none that doeth good". The Lord speaks to me, to remind me of where I came from, and of the abominations that have been brought forth in this world through me in my absence from Him. He reminds me of this; not to break my spirit, or cause resentments from within, but to show me love. From where I stand now, my righteous actions serve as a testimony to His saving grace. The fact that a former pit dweller now writes furiously of his Lord's glory is but praise to His power. The Lord has saved me from myself. Transformation so profound only comes from one source: <u>HIM</u>! To recover (though we never do fully) from the disease of addiction is such a profound transformation. Our loved ones see it and rejoice, simply because they can finally breathe. Holding their breath in anticipation of our deaths has made them weary. God raises His hand to bless us, for we have taken the steps toward purifying ourselves. He sees us take the gift of life that He has given us, and to begin to treat it with respect and appreciation. Lord, I can not speak enough of how Your lowly child has come to love Thy gifts; for they are plenty, and no longer disguised by my iniquities as anything other than Your love for me.

Psalm 54

As I step out into the world each day, I must be mindful that, though my path is pure under His guidance, there are still spiritual enemies out there. The world is not a perfect place, because man has made it imperfect. We dwell here, both with our brethren, as well as those who would assail us. My faith may be assaulted by people or things, and I must be prepared. We (my guides and I) pray for strength each morning. "May the Lord take you. May He walk with you, talk with you, help you carry His words to others. And may He bring you home safe and sound, in Jesus' name". This prayer is one of the first things I hear each and every day. It helps to send me out into life amongst the wolves and sheep, and I fear not. The wolves are kept at bay by my faith, yet, they strike down the weakest of the sheep. Your faith can only be challenged if it is weak. As I commune each day with the Lord, and my guides, my faith grows stronger. As I write, and see how quickly and diligently He works through me, my faith grows stronger. As I watch myself grow healthier in body and spirit, my faith grows stronger. One day, when I lay my head down for the last time, and prepare to leave this world, not a throng of wolves at my bedside could keep my soul from its rightful destination!

Psalm 55

As I read Psalm 55, I nearly laughed. It amazes me how simply one Psalm, only 23 verses, basically sums up the entire story of my journey until now. Psalm 55:2 says: "Attend unto me, and hear me: I mourn in my complaint, and make a noise;". Oh my: how great I had gotten at complaining, and how entitled I felt to have my complaints heard; for, surely, I was the only person in the world with any true worth, and that gave me privilege. I could declare God false, but then bend His ear with my woes; for I had none other who wanted to listen. HA! Psalm 55:13-14 says: "But it was thou, a man mine equal, my guide, and mine acquaintance. We took sweet counsel together, and walked unto the house of God in company". It's almost as if the Psalms have dictated the path I was to follow, though created so long ago. I did just such a thing, nearly word for word. This book is a result of that. Ahh! The book and the words speak to me ever clearer with every verse. I can see myself in these teachings. I learn and grow and, oh, by God and His will, I am recovering! I did not drink today. Instead I read, and I wrote, and I learned. I thirst not for the bottle, but, instead, I quench my cleansed pallet with teachings of glorious proportions! My being is filled with happiness, for I am changing! And, for the first time, changing for the better.

Psalm 56

There is a particular part of this Psalm that has really struck me. The last part of the last verse of Psalm 56:13 says: "wilt not thou deliver my feet from falling, that I may walk before God in the light of the living?" Powerful is the thought: to walk before God in the light of the living! To be an example of the Lord on this earth! To walk the path of the anointed! To <u>STAY</u> sober, and to use the power of the afflicted and diseased to <u>SAVE</u>! Through God, and His ability to turn my will to good, shall this be done; for it is His will. Deliver my feet from falling. Think of falling, or tripping, for that matter. Your feet are the only part that do not actually hit the ground, for that is where they were when you began falling. He speaks more of falling down, through this place, into the pit. Keep your path righteous, and you shall not feel the sting upon your soles; for you shall not plummet to join the fallen! I shall not join them! I had my ticket stamped and approved; and I've traded away my boarding pass for a one way journey to the land of the forsaken. I now crave to one day feel air beneath my wings; to be able to wield spear or sword against the enemy; to defend the Kingdom of my Savior; for it is high, and it is holy. I crave, but I will not seek out of vanity, for His plan for me is still being revealed.

Psalm 57

To be able to rejoice in knowing that God's wings shall encompass me in my time of calamity is a true blessing. Even now, as I sit and wait to head out into the world to be judged by my fellows, He protects me. I bear no fear, and my hands do not shake in anticipation of the unknown. I have faith that, on this day, as every day, He goes with me. I dread not, for I own all of my wrongs; and in doing so, He will protect me. Psalm 57:7 says: "My heart is fixed, O God, my heart is fixed: I will sing and give praise." Faith and trust in the Lord has allowed me to walk this day with strength and courage. I have sinned, both against the Lord, and against my fellow man; and today, I must answer to the lesser. May my fellows judge me true, for God is within me, and He now guides me. May they see that their brother is changing, that he is growing, and that he now walks a righteous path. May God grant unto them mercy toward me; for I am truly sorry, and I own my wrongs. I fret not, for this is all part of His plan for me; a part of the path that He has deemed I must walk. I fear not the pebbles that will be strewn along my road, for my destination is pure and just.

Psalm 58

There are many things of this earth which are sent out with but one purpose: to lead us astray. It could be a person, a place, or a thing. It could be a substance, like drugs or alcohol, it could be a lover, or it could be a "friend". It could even be a family member. Psalm 58:5 says: "Which will not hearken to the voice of the charmers, charming never so wisely". My charmer has always been alcohol; baffling me with its ability to talk me out of remembering all of the damage, all of the tears, all of the brokenness that I was still fixing. "Don't think about that time, you know, where all that stuff happened. Don't remember those feelings. Just remember how good I felt against your lips, and the warmth of oblivion". God knows how cunning the tongue of my foe is. And there is no escape, because my foe is part of me, buried so deep that it can never be fully removed. However, for the first time in my life, as this foe tries to sway me day to day, all I hear is a muffled struggle. God has His hand over the mouth of mine enemy, so I shall not hear its lies. As each day passes, it is drowning in its own filth, and it can no longer spew it forth to my ears. This is a gift from the Lord: to silence my enemy, so my mind may have peace.

Psalm 59

As I sat today, and waited for the judgment from my fellow men, I found myself in a new frame of mind, which I hadn't before experienced. In the past, I would look around, and see a room full of my enemies, who had gathered to watch me receive the justice of men. I would see the ones sent to argue against me, the ones sent to judge my earthly fate, the ones sent to shackle me and take me away. Today I saw none of those. I sat on a bench, enveloped by my faith in the Lord, and waited. My mind was at perfect ease, my soul was content in His embrace. I watched others be judged, shackled, and taken away; but my faith did not waver. As I was called to receive judgment, I arose and stood, humbled, and without pride. I was forgiven. The Lord had blessed me, by allowing His children to see the good in me, to see the change in me. Their judgment was guided through His will. "He has work to do, so he cannot be restrained". I can only imagine that this is the message that He delivered unto them. To assume to know His plan is not part of who this lowly man is anymore. Whatever He did today, I give thanks and praise; not for what He has given me, but, rather, that He has deemed that the work I am to do for Him is more important. Oh, how He strengthens my resolve, and, oh, how He fills my heart!

Psalm 60

Where I once turned to man for salvation, I now turn to God. I cannot say that turning to our fellows in recovery is wrong; for, as I've said, it kept me sober for two and a half years. I would never discourage another of the afflicted like myself when they pursue the fellowship of recovery, for it is good. Whether you believe in God or not, to want to help bring an end to the suffering of another human being is a righteous cause. It is possible to do God's work without even believing that you are. It's almost humorous. It seems to me that He has plans for all of us. I managed to stay sober through this fellowship; but, for me, it was temporary relief. I ended up with one bottle in my hand, then two bottles; until I was hanging my head in remorse. While I had allowed my fellows to help change my thought processes, to help me fight my demons, I was ignoring the deeper root of the problem. I had a dirty soul, a lack of faith. Enemies met me at every turn, and I perceived them as enemies; but I lacked the strength to face them, and strike them down. Even with my fellows, I was fighting this battle alone, and I was losing. With all the armies of the Lord gathered behind me now, I am truly ready for battle. It <u>WILL</u> be a battle, but I <u>WILL</u> be victorious; For <u>HE</u> has told me so!

Psalm 61

In my time of crisis, I will, nay, I <u>MUST</u>, turn to the Lord, for He is the only One Who can alleviate the pains associated with struggle. Anxiety will be lifted, and worry will be banished from my mind, as He can heal all these ailments of conscious thought, and all of these iniquities of my thought process and perception. I'm feeble, and I cannot cope alone with all the transgressions brought forth unto me by the ones who seek to be my undoing, and to drive me back to my best-known and most vile coping skill . . . With faith and trust in Him I fear not these things. I have noticed that, since I accepted the Lord, these feelings, if anything at all, have become nothing more than fleeting experiences. They're like a brief handshake with the enemy, and then they're gone. God, in His infinite wisdom, wipes them away, as if but dust on the counter. Maybe I have spent enough time wallowing in these feelings. Maybe I have learned the lessons from them that I had been destined to. Regardless, they plague me not. He feels that I do not need to experience these emotions, because they serve no purpose in His plan for me. That is the best explanation I can muster, if I try to reason it out. I thank Him for this, for it makes my life good. <u>HE</u> makes my life good. He does not fail me; and, with diligence and perseverance, I shall not fail Him.

Psalm 62

There is a verse in Psalm 62 that speaks to me profoundly. Psalm 62:10 says: "Trust not in oppression, and become not vain in robbery: if riches increase, set not your heart upon them". Only God knows what my future holds for me. Whether I am destined to live out my life as a pauper, or to have material wealth, I must keep my eyes on the prize. I must hold the Lord above all else that I may have, for He is, and shall always be, my greatest joy. His presence in my life cannot be weighed in gold, nor given a dollar value. No amount of money or possessions in the past have brought me to this place of peace. They, in fact, have only brought with them the displeasures that outweighed their value. I desire not these things, and take solace in knowing that the Lord shall give me exactly what I need. He has an inventory planned out, and times in which they shall be delivered to me. He knows that one of my biggest faults was judging my recovery by my material gains. He has blessed me with a new perspective with righteous sight. My success in recovery is determined by my growth, both spiritually, and in my thought processes. As these change, so do my actions. My wants and needs differ from before. They are just; and HE is the reason, and I praise Him for this.

Psalm 63

Each day as I awake, I am immediately reminded of the Lord's presence in my life. He has put this into me, so that I may be strengthened before my head even leaves the pillow. When I was sober in the past, I often spoke of how my mornings were so vague. I'd wake, get ready for work, and I was out the door in ten minutes. I'd drive to work and begin my day, and several hours later, I would finally actually "wake up". "Autopilot", I would jest with my friends. As I look back now, I see how this was actually a sign that I was ill. I had no greater force driving me. I was simply existing. I was living a godless existence, riddled with moments like the one that I just described; like I was a shell of something that, in the beginning, had been planned to be better, but was never finished. I was a shell that had never been filled. Again, we come to the infinite void that only HE can fill. Filling this void in recovery is ever so important, for it is that space that our disease craves to call home. "Let ME fill it!", it cries to us at every turn. Oh, how smitten with jealousy my disease has become, as it watches its former home become the dwelling of the Lord. Foreclosed upon by His will, HE has made it His own. And with that, I sing, and dance the dance of joy; no longer keeping the beast at bay through the use of other beasts. HE is all I need.

Psalm 64

We, the afflicted, bring upon our own heads all that we have suffered. We must remember that, even though we have a disease, our disease is <u>PART</u> of us. It is built in, part of who we are. It is both a learned practice, and an inherent one; be it genetic, or simply neuropathways that have been formed due to our life-long abuse of substances. Science has many explanations for our ailment. But, whether it's science, or the fellowship, or God, we, nonetheless, <u>MUST</u> own that this is our disease. Psalm 64:8 says: "So they shall make their own tongue to fall upon themselves: all that see them shall flee away". Though we are ill, and our substances lead us to ill decisions, and then rob us of the memory of them, we have to own our actions; for they were performed by our hands, and spoken by our tongues. Staying away from substances allows us to make better decisions, and, in so doing, we (hopefully) perform better actions. Accepting God has allowed me to accept myself. The wrongs that I have done are mine, and they belong to no one else. Knowing this gives me the courage to stand amongst those I have wronged, head held high. I am changing for the better. If they judge me, that is their right; for God gave them free will. If they choose not to forgive, that is their right, too; for God <u>GAVE</u> them free will. I will accept either course they choose to take, for I have given <u>MY</u> will back to God, and He has asked me to forgive and to forget. The past serves a purpose. It made me who I am today, and taught me lessons. But tomorrow's purposes have a deeper profoundness, for He has made me feel it.

Psalm 65

Psalm 65 speaks praise to the Lord for all the gifts of the land which He has given to us. This is a profound realization for someone who had taken these things for granted his entire life. I had found myself standing in front of a place of worry yesterday morning. As I waited to be allowed inside I found myself staring off down a hill. I studied where the road ended, and the tree line began. The trees were bare from the frost, and I could see through them, and to the hill behind them. As the hill grew steeper, I could see beautiful homes that lay scattered about the side of it. And, at the crest of the hill, I saw the sun as it was beginning its journey across the sky. I can't remember the last time I had just stopped to appreciate the beauty around me. I was in a place where I should have been afraid; but, instead, I found myself full of mindfulness. I was staying present in the moment. I was appreciating the beauty of God's creation in front of me, rather than fretting over my situation, and forecasting my day. At total peace with the world around me, I knew that I was meant to be in that place right at that particular point in time. I was meant to enjoy that view, to behold its beauty, even though I did not WANT to be there. My wants, if my past is to be a lesson, are incorrect. His are perfect.

Psalm 66

As we learn to survive in recovery, there are many parts of our thought process that must change. I know that I have many misleading perceptions that threaten to bring me back into a dangerous mind set. With God, I find these changes rather easy compared to my previous attempts without Him. Psalm 66:12 says: "Thou hast caused men to ride over our heads; we went through fire and through water: but thou broughtest us out into a wealthy place". All of our sufferings and trials through our active addictions may seem, at first glance, to be misfortunes. They are hard to look back on, for the memories bring with them pain. But, as I learn to look back and appreciate the lessons that I have been given, it robs these memories of their power over my will. I will not be allowed by the Lord to dwell on these things, for He knows it is not healthy for me, and it is not where He wants my mind. He has graced me with new things to focus on and to direct my energy towards. In His infinite wisdom, He has decided which things I am to hold onto, and which I am to discard. He washes my soul of the sin, for He knows that I have repented of my past wrongs. This leaves me in a place of peace from which to conduct <u>HIS</u> work.

Psalm 67

Psalm 67 speaks of all of the people of the earth rejoicing in God's glory and having a fruitful existence as a united people under Him. It is a very unselfish Psalm. While some speak of personal deliverance, or seek out God's wrath upon the wicked, Psalm 67 simply asks that all of His people be made to be happy. It is touching. I am reminded that recovery is both a selfish and a giving practice. We must be selfish when it comes to situations where our sobriety could be jeopordized. We must refuse generous invitations to events we deem could be hazardous through temptation. We need to distance ourselves from toxic people. We sometimes need to fight our demons first, and to put others second; all the while remembering that, if we go back to active addiction, we're useless to others. The giving aspect of recovery (you can only keep it by giving it away) is helping others who suffer. This, in and of itself, can be considered a selfish act, simply because it feels good, and helping others ultimately helps ourselves. However, the good that is done in our pursuits to help others far outweighs the selfish aspect. We give our time, we give our words, and we let God act through us to try and save. If we change the life of another, there is no telling the impact it may have on others that they themselves may touch and help. Like the domino effect, initiated by God, so many lives can be impacted by His words, even if delivered by just one person. People we may never meet may be introduced to sobriety, and to God, through OUR actions today. That's called a miracle.

Psalm 68

I cannot understand the doings of God, for I was not meant to. His power is so great and so vast that my simple being can do nothing but experience it. Like being in a river with an overpowering current, trying to swim against it is pointless; for the river <u>IS</u> going to take you and deposit you where you were meant to be. I can see that, all my life, I have been in this river, clinging to a feeble branch from a shoreline tree, and trying to resist the current. After letting go, I have found myself with a new peace. I drift; and, as I do, I am finally experiencing life, as though for the first time. Through my readings of His Word, I have found countless testimonies of His powers over this life, and the next, and how every life is impacted by His will. Thus, I write my own testimonies of being saved as I hurdled down the corridors of death. The most amazing part is that I do this sober, and with no desire to drink! To the average person who does not struggle with addiction, this may not seem like much; but, to one of the afflicted like myself, this is amazing! A miracle! Nothing can unmake me as an alcoholic. But God has lifted my desire to drink, or to commune with my nemesis in any way. Oh, how I drift in His river, and travel farther from that wretched place where I clung to the branch for so long. And I'll never return!

Psalm 69

I am reminded that, even though I may face many enemies in my recovery, it is even more important to be able to identify <u>WHO</u> is actually my enemy, and who are my friends. The disease of addiction most certainly clouds our judgment. When we are actively using anyone who tries to step in and help, we're automatically perceiving them to be a foe; for they want to take from us that which we crave most at that time: our substance. Though they mean well, we are blind to their intent, because our focus is on ourselves at all times. Even when sober, and the fog of intoxication is lifted, we can still have these misconceptions. People ask us, and even try to force us, to attend treatment. We may not want to go, and we feel that we do not need it. The same goes for meetings. We may be asked if we attend, and we receive stern suggestions, if we don't. Therefore, since they are pushing us towards something that we do not <u>WANT</u>, they are working against us. This is the disease still controlling our thought processes. Even sober it takes hold. It doesn't want us in treatment, and it doesn't want us to go to meetings. It wants us alone, in our own heads, where it can corner us. In my new-found faith, I am relieved of these misconceptions. God has shown me who my friends are, as well as my foes. I was struck with the urge to put myself in treatment, and to talk with at least one addict or alcoholic about recovery each day. God stands with me, so that I will never again be alone with my disease. I will never again cower in the corner of my mind as it takes hold.

Psalm 70

Psalm 70:5 says: "But I am poor and needy: make haste unto me, O God: thou art my help and my deliverer; O Lord, make no tarrying". Transitioning from active addiction to sobriety leaves the vast majority of us confused, ill, poor, both materially and spiritually, weak, fragile, and, of course, remorseful. These things cause very many of us to return to our substance for comfort. It is too much to bear in the beginning, and we just want it to go away. "I want what I want, and I want it now". Instant gratification is the way of the afflicted mind. For some inexplicable reason, God deemed that I not feel these things but for a brief moment after my last relapse. He let me experience the emotions for a short while, and then He touched me, and they were gone. "Now it is time to focus on work". Though these words were not spoken to me directly, I felt as though they were. A force inside of me began to drive me forward in my faith, and I found a peace that I had never felt before in my entire life. I had been graced by the Lord with a clean mind; one that had been cleansed of all things that would stop it from doing the Lord's work. Oh, how amazing and wondrous this feeling! I pursue it now with the same intensity that I had pursued that which would have destroyed me. It consumes me in a light that blinds me to the darkness of my past.

Psalm 71

Recovery has its ups and downs, much like most things in life. There are days which we perceive as good, and those we see as bad. Challenges await, there is no doubt, for they lie in wait for us. And sometimes, it IS hard to stay strong; for we are human. Psalm 71:9 says: "Cast me not off in the time of old age; forsake me not when my strength faileth". With God in my life, I can find solace, knowing that, as long as I have faith, He will be there with me, even in my times of weakness. And those times ARE inevitable. In the rooms and in treatment, we often hear that relapse is a part of recovery, and that we learn something new each time, that better prepares us to avoid another. But relapse doesn't HAVE to be a part of recovery. We CAN choose to never use or drink again. But how? This Psalm reminds me that I have a powerful medicine in the Lord that will be there for me when the struggle becomes real. God willing, I will never pick up another drink, so long as I breathe. I keep my eyes on the Lord, and do not lose sight; for I know that, as soon as I do, my disease will pounce upon me like a lion. I know that, even at my weakest points, my most vulnerable moments, I can persevere, and avoid relapse, simply by keeping Him in my heart.

Psalm 72

Recovery is not easy, nor is life in general. But, if we walk a righteous path, we walk with the knowledge that we are doing good things. This is powerful in sobriety. Knowing that, from one step to the next, you have done the right thing, and made the correct decisions, bolsters our confidence in ourselves. Self-confidence is important; not to the point of a swelled ego, but simply to the state of being where temptations are not so tempting. Psalm 72:14 says: "He shall redeem their soul from deceit and violence: and precious shall their blood be in his sight". God has redeemed my soul. More accurately, He has judged it, and found it to be just. In His grace, He has purified it, cleansed my sins, and given me direction. I make better decisions under His watchful tending. And though I will most certainly bleed at some point in the future, my blood is precious in the eyes of the Lord; for He made it, and He keeps it pure. This blood that courses through me keeps my physical being moving about and helping others. It keeps my fingers moving as I write, and my mind going as I read. It delivers throughout my body all that I need, as I pray that the words that I have written will help another. Even if I help just one, I would be successful in my purpose.

Psalm 73

We who recover have become all too familiar with our physical ailments in the transition into abstinence. However, a much-overlooked aspect of the process is our spiritual ones. Today, as I sit here, and am filled with the Lord's favour, I can testify of my own spiritual failures. At my worst, I would wake up early, and begin drinking immediately, to stay the effects of detoxing. I was fully intoxicated (black out) before I could finish watching one movie. I would awake several hours later, and repeat the process, over and over. What kind of existence is that? Where is the spirituality in this situation? It was in the bottle. Hence the name "spirits". A falsehood, a false god, a fake life. I was dying, slowly killing myself with alcohol; and the root of that problem was my lack of anything spiritual in my life. Though God was there, I would not let Him in. Like friends who would come to take my bottles away, I'd lock the door, and be as quiet as I could until they went away. I did the same with God. I locked Him out, until I thought that He had gone away. But He never left! Instead, He sent a barrage of His soldiers with the orders to take me away from the bottles, with force, if necessary. He sent His speakers to fill my ears with their voices, and He sent His servants to aid my transition. He did all of this, for me, to save me! I have many debts, but none so great as that of the one I owe the Lord.

Psalm 74

Challenges, tribulations, or tests? Perception is the key. You can wallow in self-pity during an onslaught, or you can stand firm in defiance. It is but a choice, a choice fueled by faith in God and faith in ourselves. Self-righteous warriors will accost our faith; but, stand firm, brothers. Self-proclaimed life experts will assault our sobriety; but, stand firm, brothers. Educated non-believers will laugh in our faces; but, stand firm, I say. Victims of our addictions will watch and wait for us to fail; but, oh, how we do stand so firmly. God is a powerful Force, holding us ever so steady as we endure these attacks. May peace fall upon us as our assailants await our tears. Be strong, I say, as my Lord has told me to be. Fear cannot grip me, for God has made me slippery to his grasp. Pity shall not encompass me, for it has no place upon my head. Frailty of spirit shall never call my soul home. And mercy shall be delivered unto my enemy's ears from my lips, so that they may weep in their ways when they see I cannot be toppled. This shall be, for it is part of my path. To be blessed with this level of understanding, of how the Lord can make such monumental changes within such a short period of time, is heavenly. Not many get to experience it, and those who do are truly blessed; for they have been chosen to be messengers.

Psalm 75

The world is in a state of constant change. God's workings within it are mysterious, for they were meant to be that way. We take for granted that things will always be the same; but, at any time, they can change, by the Lord's will. Accepting these changes is critical to staying spiritually in tune with the Lord. It is also critical to prevent falling back into old trains of thought, and ultimately, a possible relapse. Losing a job, a close friend moving away, losing a loved one. The list of life-altering changes is nearly endless, and we will all experience some of these events at some point in our lives. A strong support network is key. For myself, I put the Lord as the Head of this network; for everyone else in it was brought to me by Him. I can call Him any time I wish, with no need for a phone, and He always answers. He is never too busy to talk, and He will never rush me away. He does not cater to my ego, but He never puts me down. He hears my words, He sees my tears, and He replaces them with a smile; for He is good. When I need, and my need is just, He provides, and I do not go without. When I want, and my wants are vain, I do not receive, and I <u>LEARN</u>. I know that, now, I am being taught and trained. In this way, when the world around me changes, I will be better equipped by Him to accept and drive on; for He has deemed that I shall not be weakened by His doings, because they are perfect.

Psalm 76

The Lord holds reign over all that occurs in this life. To struggle to control the world around me is actually to work against the Lord's will. I see this now. Regardless of our place here, be it poor, or of royalty, we all ultimately stand in front of the same Judge in the end. Looking forward to this event keeps me better rooted in the present, and more mindful of the goings on in it. Mindfulness is a blessing in recovery; whether you stop to enjoy a view, savor the taste of a delicious meal, or enjoy a conversation with a loved one. Staying where we are, and attending to the present, keeps us from forecasting and dwelling on negative things, and saying to ourselves, "if only this had been different, or this had gone differently." These thoughts cloud our minds with "what if's", ultimately keeping us away from reality in the moment. Spending a lifetime in my fantasy realm of what COULD have been has robbed me of the simple pleasures of the present. Now, as a servant of the Lord, I live day to day, never looking too far ahead. We say in recovery: "one day at a time". Very good advice; for that's all the Lord asks of us. Take it day by day, get up and walk a good path. Moment by moment be kind and generous. Living this way, my days are filled with peace and prosperity of spirit. And it feels oh, so good!

Psalm 77

Psalm 77:2-4 says: "In the day of my trouble I sought the Lord: my sore ran in the night, and ceased not; my soul refused to be comforted. I remembered God, and was troubled: I complained, and my spirit was overwhelmed. Selah. Thou holdest mine eyes waking: I am so troubled that I cannot speak". How many nights have we laid awake, our minds awash with worries? Reaching out from within to God, asking for help? Believers and non-believers alike, we have all prayed in our darkest moments, either consciously or subconsciously. Regardless if our prayers were just or blasphemous in nature, we had some kind of urge to acknowledge God as real. Desperation for ourselves, though rooted in vanity, can lead to salvation. It's a change of mind that occurs, once you truly find the Lord. Though self-preservation may lead you to Him, it is the gift of the righteous soul that keeps you willingly in His embrace. Our wants and prayers eventually transition from the selfish to the selfless. Even now, fairly early in my recovery and my spirituality, I find myself asking for less and less to happen in my own life. I ask more for the blessings upon others. People who I know are struggling with things fill my prayers each day. Other than asking for the Lord to guide me each day, I am absent from my prayers. An evolution in selflessness is occurring within me by His will, and it is glorious!

Psalm 78

As many of my brothers lead a godless existence, whether they're atheist or agnostic, I can testify to the loneliness and lack of guidance that accompanies these; for that is the place from which I came. I do not judge them; rather, oh, how I do love them, for they are my brothers and sisters. Some are perfectly content in their ways; but, once again, I do not judge. My brethren in recovery, however, know all too well of what I speak. In addiction, we grow farther away from a healthy lifestyle. Gradually, we become more and more ill, until we are blessed with recovery. In many ways, society has the same ailment. We, as a people, have grown farther and farther away from righteousness as the years have passed. We fight unjust wars, we give to ill causes, we pursue vanity at a blistering pace. But, looking at society's laws and regulations now, you can still see the influence of God's teachings. We still hold many of His laws as our own. However, we have grown farther and farther from the purity of His law, watering it down with amendments to satisfy our own lusts. In finding God, I have had many new insights into what is right and wrong; possibly most important of those being that I am to stay sober. He <u>NEEDS</u> me to stay sober. He has asked that of me in the past, but I amended His requests with exceptions. That is a thing that I will do no more.

Psalm 79

Throughout our lives, we find ourselves admiring others for what they may have, whether it be riches, a successful marriage, a great job, happiness in general, or, in the case of us who struggle with the disease of addiction, sober time. Admiration, while fairly good in its intentions, can be the catalyst for jealousy. Jealousy begets coveting, and then coveting begets ill thoughts and intentions. We can look at another, and say: "Why does he have so much, and me so little?" This train of thinking leads us back to the darkness of self-pity, and breeds loathing for those who have what we do not; drawing us farther from spiritual soundness, and thus from the Lord. In recovery, it takes our focus away from the incredible accomplishment of being sober <u>IN</u> <u>SPITE</u> of things we may feel we lack. It is amazing how the transition of our thoughts proceeds when we get sober. At first, all we want to do is to stop using. "If I can just do this, then I'll be happy forever". Then it's the car. "All I need is this, and I'll be happy forever". Then it's the romance. "If I can only find the right one, I'll be happy forever". The want spiral never ends. With the Lord, I know these things will come as He sees fit. I do not wait on them or pursue them. He has granted me total peace in just knowing that I have sobriety, and I have Him.

Psalm 80

I am reminded that struggles will always be a part of life; and mine are far from over. God willing, I will live a long and full life, which ultimately means that there will be times of turmoil; for that is just how things are. Having the disease of addiction alone means I will have a daily foe to keep in check for the rest of my time here. However, these are things that I will never have to face alone. I am excited to overcome any challenge, any oppressor. My new-found strength through faith gives me the confidence to persevere. I have Someone to reach out to at any given time, to ask for guidance and ruggedness. The doubters would look at this as medicating an illness with a placebo, for they do not believe. But I will say, "Look at me, I am well even though I am diseased". I face struggles, but I do not struggle through them. Instead, I stride, pure of heart and calm of mind, through situations that seek to eliminate my faith. That is ultimately all that is required to begin the journey into God's favour. The other aspects come with time and knowledge of His Word; but, without faith, all is lost. It's a keystone, if you will. Remove it, and the structure topples. Instead, bolster it with the mortar of righteous deeds. Help another who suffers. Love those who love you, and love those who do not. Speak freely of God's amazing impact on your life, for it is, oh, so surely His.

Psalm 81

False gods plague us in today's societies. Sometimes they are not all too clear, and we are not even aware of the pedestals we erect in their honor. Celebrities, politicians, material objects, <u>SUBSTANCES</u>. These all have battled in our lives to be placed on pedestals. We who struggle with addiction know the lengths at which we would go to in order to acquire and be with our substance of choice. We have stolen, we have sold precious possessions, we have done favors for those who dwell in the pit. There was literally no end to what we were capable of, for our desire was that deep and uncontrollable. I once had a clinician tell me that, if he owned a business, he would hire nothing but addicts and alcoholics in recovery, because they have no limit to their abilities, and will apply themselves to a task with a furious energy until it is accomplished. It makes perfect sense to someone in recovery, but not so much to someone who has not experienced addiction. False gods will do nothing but ultimately take us down with them when they have inevitably fallen off of their pedestals. That is why I have placed the true Lord on mine, and removed all others. He cannot fall, and He will never fail me. He cannot be held below another, for none other can do what He does. Life is a whole lot simpler with a true Higher Power. I only have to give praise and thanks to One, and He is God.

Psalm 82

Psalm 82:3 says: "Defend the poor and fatherless: do justice to the afflicted and needy". God favours those of us who have suffered. He who knows all has seen our struggles and has counted our tears. He does not rejoice in our pain, nor does He smile upon our bloodshed. He loves all of us who are His children. Justice to the afflicted in my life has been all the things the Lord has done for me since I let Him into my life. He has given me guides and guardian angels a-plenty. He has sent even non-believers to aid me in my journey of righteousness. He has stopped my tears, for He has said no more. He has healed my wounds, for He has said that He does not wish to see my blood anywhere but in my veins. Those who have endured no suffering can never fully appreciate how monumental an occurrence this is. In recovery, we see this quite often. In treatment, we work with people who simply have an education on addiction. Their words seem as if drawn from textbooks, and we know that their bottom line is a paycheck. They have grown weary of the same faces, and have long since lost the urge to help. We can see this, as if a sign is hung about their neck. Then there are those who have suffered and are trying to help others. A passion is about them, for they <u>KNOW</u> our pain. We shut up, and listen. We respect their experience, and try to learn. God works much the same way. He knows the afflicted and the poor have suffered. When we speak, He listens intently. He knows we have sacrificed, and we need only to reach out to Him to be saved.

Psalm 83

Throughout life's journey there will be many who seem to conspire against us for our belief in God. Just as in recovery, there will be those who pass judgment on us, because we have a "filthy" disease; a disease of the mind that many do not even consider to be an illness, but, rather, a string of conscious ill choices. Even the non-believers struggle with the scientific explanation of the illness, though many hold science as their deity. These are all but challenges to both our faith, and our recovery. I have found that, with strong faith, it also does wonders to bolster my recovery. There are those in my daily life who I can still catch throwing distasteful glances my way. My faith in God immediately turns these things that would make me feel lowly into positives, and I smile. Smile in the face of my oppressors. "They have no idea", I simply tell myself, and I move forward. I pity those who seek my envy. I look down upon the heads of those who would place themselves above me. I stare eye to eye with the just and righteous. God has given me this. Let them pass judgment on me, Lord. Let them cast words as bricks, and let them see how those fall ever so short of the mark. For when the day has ended, and I prepare for the night's sleep, I smile. Each and every night I do smile.

Psalm 84

Psalm 84:11 says: "For the Lord God is a sun and shield: the Lord will give grace and glory: no good thing will he withhold from them that walk uprightly". All of the best things that are to come in this life and in the next are obtained through living well, in spirit and body and mind. To walk uprightly is to be just. To keep the Lord first and to be kind and gentle to others. I had spent the majority of my life trying to be kind to others, when I was sober. I did it simply because I felt I did not want to be mean. Little did I know that, deep inside of me, there was a soldier of the Lord struggling to get out. Deep down, I was a good person, even though I was fluent in self-destruction. This does not dirty my soul now. Instead of seeing spirituality as a sudden flip of a light switch, I see it that this has been a change that has been occurring in me for quite some time. There had always been a deeper meaning to my being. It took a long time to discover it, but even at my worst moments, it was within me somewhere. In a way, I think that, during its struggle to have itself be known, it had clashed with my lifestyle and mind set at the time, leaving me confused and vulnerable. Now that my spirituality has consumed me and cast out the wretchedness, I can finally be as I was meant to be: kind, gentle, loving, peaceful, meek, humble, and by the grace of the Lord, righteous.

Psalm 85

Having been raised Roman Catholic, I had been brought up to believe that, to atone for your sins, you must go to confession. As I grew older, and had forsaken any religion, I would often think to myself in jest: "Boy if I ever go back to confess I'll have a laundry list as long as a novel to bring". I often catch myself, in both speaking and writing, talking about needing to atone for the things I have done. My guides each time assure me that I do not. They tell me that the Lord knows that I am remorseful, and that, by simply living His way, and accepting Him, I am forgiven. I do not hold any of my previous sins in my heart; so, by letting them go, and by letting God in, I have been cleansed of my wrongs. I can see this, simply by watching my values change. I want different things than I did before. I take pleasure in good things, and do not pursue evils. Most importantly, I no longer value the state of drunkenness. Even with a couple years sober, I would crave the bottle. Now, under the direction of the Lord, I couldn't be farther from picking up another drink. I have no spots left on my soul from which I feel I need to hide. There are no assaults that will turn me to alcohol, for the Lord shall walk with me through them. There is no darkness left within me, for God has cast His light. I want to share this feeling with the world. I want those who suffer to experience it and to be saved.

Psalm 86

Psalm 86:13 says: "For great is thy mercy toward me: and thou hast delivered my soul from the lowest hell". One of the hardest parts of recovery, substantially more so in the beginning, is looking back on the hell from which we came. It can be overwhelming. The things we did we cannot believe. The remorse runs so deep for the people we hurt. We lost so many things that we held so dear, simply because of the way we lived, moment to moment, dwelling in a cesspool of evils and filth. For myself, I would think of sitting on my couch, watching movies. I would get up to take a shot, then return to the couch. The blinds were drawn, and my apartment was dark, though it was noon. Before the burn had left my throat, I would be up and heading for the next sip. A semi-conscious state enveloped me, and I could not remember, nor consciously stop myself. I would get "inspired" by my suffering and pick up my guitar, only to find my fingers had no direction. They too, had lost their memory. This is my hell on earth. Not the legal problems, nor the things lost, nor the relationships broken. Just simply being there, under the control of a vile substance, unable to stop myself; a prisoner in my own body and mind. The disease weakened me to the point where, even though I walked about, my soul was asleep. If hell can exist on earth in such a fashion, I pray to God to be delivered from experiencing the hell of the next life!

Psalm 87

Psalm 87:1 says: "His foundation is in the holy mountains". Though it may not have been the intent of this Psalm, this verse has gotten me thinking. In spirituality, as well as in recovery, where we lay our foundations is very important. I have laid both of mine down in the Lord, for He is doing wonders for me in both aspects. For recovery's sake, we must build our foundations on something that is more powerful than ourselves, our higher power. In the past, when we build our foundations upon ourselves, or on vain things, our houses have toppled. I chose God as my Higher Power, because I cannot perceive of anything more powerful than He Who has made all that is. It is not my place to push God on anyone, but it is my place, as a recovering alcoholic, to testify that there is a dire need to admit we are not the most powerful forces in our own lives. Being humble is part of the first step, by admitting powerlessness over our substance. This automatically admits your substance is a higher power, and, thus, we cannot fight it alone. The only way to take that power away from our drug of choice is to find something more powerful than IT, and hold on to that for dear life. It can be the fellowship, a sponsor, a charity, our family, or many other things. But keep in mind that not all work; and, from time to time, we may need to rethink our choices in a higher power. God will always be there, and will always be more powerful than me or my alcohol. He is THE perfect Higher Power.

Psalm 88

Through this Psalm, I am reminded of the healing power of prayer. Though it speaks of being forsaken and cast away, it speaks of prayer, and of crying out to the Lord. I pray each day, both through the good days and the bad; whereas, in the past, I would only pray when I wanted, or when I felt assailed. To wake each morning, and to begin the day with a prayer of thanks, is both humbling and fulfilling. It's like taking medicine for the soul in the morning. Just knowing that I spoke to the Lord, and have been given His blessing on this day, serves to make me strong to walk amongst my brothers, amongst my enemies, and walk with my demons; for they reside within me. Though I may always have the iniquitous monster inside of me, through the power of prayer, it remains chained and bound. The Lord has come down and subdued the beast hastily. It cowers in His presence; and, for the first time, experiences fear, which is a new experience for it. He has cast divine chains about the vile creature, which no man nor demon can break. If the beast should attempt to take an upper hand once again, it would have to remove God from my life; and that will not happen! I shall no longer run from the Lord, for He is good; and He will never abandon me. He has told me through His loving embrace that He is not going anywhere. For I am His son, and He loves me so.

Psalm 89

Perseverance in both faith and abstinence from substances can be challenging, but are more than worthwhile. God, in His endless mercy, is always willing to forgive, if we return to Him with pure hearts, and sorrow for our misdoings; keeping in mind, however, that He is wise to the afflicted mind, and is well aware if we are not sincere. Should our faith waver, we will not, however, be forsaken. In sobriety we are taught much the same. If we "slip", or "mess up", we need to pick ourselves back up, dust ourselves off, and get back to living right. We need to go back to meetings, where we'll be welcomed, and accepted back, with open arms and no judgment. For these people know the sickness all too well, and they understand deeply. God is well aware of the challenges we face each day. While we would serve Him better with unwavering faith, it is not entirely possible for everyone. Things <u>WILL</u> happen that could potentially jeopardize it, or shake it. The important part is not to give up completely. If we relapse and give up, we die. If we lose faith and give up, we forsake eternal happiness. Both are equally terrifying. Persevere, my brothers. Though I may trip, I shall not fall, for the Lord is my net, and sobriety keeps me steady on my feet. My path is cleaned of debris by Him daily, and I pray to show this to others someday.

Psalm 90

Imagine, but for a moment, that we could have no secrets. No secret sins, no hidden agendas, no ability to mislead. We could not move about taking solace in knowing others to be ignorant of our doings. We all have our secrets. They are kept secret to all but a select few, and to the Lord. We cannot hide anything from Him, for He sees all. In active addiction, we try to hide our use from others. If they are ignorant to what is <u>REALLY</u> going on with us, then they cannot hold us accountable. That is why we promote sponsorship in recovery. It is someone who can spot our shortcomings taking hold, and help us to arrest them. It's someone who has suffered through our disease, and has a deeper knowledge of all the warning signs. It's someone to call us out when we try to keep secrets, and to hold us accountable. But what about accountability to the Lord? Sponsors, though a great asset, can be fooled. They are human, and they are far from perfect. But God is perfect, and He cannot be tricked by the likes of me, or by any other man, for that matter. Being held accountable to the Highest Authority is a very powerful tool in preventing relapse. But, alas, that again is a choice. I have to <u>CARE</u> about the Lord's opinion of me. And, for so long, I did not. Now that I care very deeply for His favor, I am held accountable for all of my actions; and I wouldn't have it any other way.

Psalm 91

I can say with an honest heart that, ever since I accepted the Lord fully, I have not known fear. I'm sure that fear is an emotion I will experience again someday, but, for now, it seems to avoid me. There have been several situations lately where I normally would have been afraid. There were things that I've had to do that fear alone may have prevented me from doing. However, it is absent. As someone who has spent his entire life gripped by fear, it's amazing how a lack of it can actually make me feel uncomfortable! I know it is just my mind adjusting to a new thought process, but it baffles me. How strong the Lord is to be able to do this for me! It is <u>ALMOST</u> fear inducing, at the risk of sounding hypocritical. Ha! I have never been a brave man. I was terrified at every twist and turn in the road. I cowered under oppression, and ran from my fears. I feared failure and loss. Now I conquer my daily doings with a bravery I've never before felt. Not an ego-driven self-pride bravery, but a God-induced courage. I <u>KNOW</u> that, if I do good to others, if I love deeply and tenderly, and if I hold God and His laws high, I have nothing to fear. I am on a predestined path, and with each step, I grow closer to Him.

Psalm 92

Do good in this life. Do good to others. For so long, I had perused all that this world has to offer, and thought to myself, "What does this world have to offer me?" I was so selfish! Those who are planted in the house of the Lord shall receive all that they desire, if not in this life, then in the next. By the same token, those who walk a righteous path do not desire the same things that the fool does. This is a new personality trait that I'm developing that is doing wonders in my recovery: wanting for <u>OTHERS</u>, rather than myself. A friend recently told me that she was ailing, and I pray for her each day. I want so desperately for her ailment to be lifted, that it's as if it was my own. Another friend has been having financial issues, and I pray for him as well. I give when I can even if it is but a small help, for that is what I want. I hear when people speak, and if their wants are just, they become <u>MY</u> wants. This is solely because I have been planted in the house of the Lord, and my soul flourishes there. I need not focus on myself (other than staying mindful of my disease), for the Lord is doing that for me. He is taking care of me, so that I may care for others. Blessed am I for being given this opportunity to give unto my fellows.

Psalm 93

The Lord has reigned since long before I came along; and He will continue to do so long after I have left this world. There have been forces at work, creating and shaping all that is since the beginning of time. This serves to remind me of how insignificant I am in the greater scheme of things. While this may sound negative at first, it is actually a <u>GOOD</u> thing. In realizing how small my place is in the big picture, I gain humbleness, powerlessness, and appreciation. Humbleness serves to keep me grounded. I don't think of myself as better than anyone else, and I crave the Lord. Powerlessness aids in my recovery. I am no longer harassed by my inner demons, because I have thrown my hands up, and admitted that I'm too weak to fight it alone. I now allow the Lord to do that <u>FOR</u> me. And appreciation. Being allowed to participate in something so much larger than me, and being given a purpose in the workings of it, is an honor. Knowing that the Lord oversees all of this, and that I may commune with Him each and every day, makes my heart swell. We exist right here, at this point in time, and at this place, for a reason. We have to try to find our purpose. Either ask the Lord for guidance, or, if you do not believe, then follow your heart. Avoid those things we know will only serve to bring us back down. Go out and do good in this world; for living a good life is a better medicine for the soul than anything the pharmacy or liquor store may have for sale.

Psalm 94

Psalm 94 (as well as many others) speaks of the battles between good and evil, the righteous and the wicked. In recovery, much as in life in general, this battle is occurring within us at all times. In addiction, we struggle with two separate personalities. Though they are within the same person, they act in opposition of one another, and they <u>HATE</u> each other. Our sober selves, and our intoxicated selves, are two separate individuals that call the same body home. They move about separately, and they seek to sabotage one another, to gain the upper hand. The sober mind, even though it was tricked by the disease into thinking it is okay to drink a <u>LITTLE</u>, will decide, "I'm just going to get a pint, its not much and I will be fine tomorrow"; trying to sabotage the disease, which craves intoxication to oblivion. The disease says, "Get a nip for the ride home, too". "Bah! Nonsense"! says the sober mind. "Drinking and driving is wrong". Two hours later, after the pint is gone, and the intoxicated mind has taken over, it becomes completely logical to drive back to the store and get more; knowing that it's sabotaging the sober mind. For, if I should get in trouble, it's the sober mind that will have to deal with the consequences. Also, by getting more booze, the odds are that I will miss work the following day, and the disease can have me again. This war is a constant, and shall remain a constant, in my life. The armies stand on opposite sides of the battleground, poised for war, to be initiated once the first sip is taken. With God as my strength, and by His will alone, the armies will grow old and bored, for that time shall not come again.

Psalm 95

God is good. We hear it from the mouths of the believers. We see it on bumper stickers. We read it in others' works. But what is that really saying? What does it mean to be good? We can say someone is good at this or good at that: that he's a good father, or she's a good mother, etc. But, an all-encompassing state of goodness? I see now that this is a trait that is reserved specifically for the Lord alone; for we are but men, perfectly imperfect. Every person has a breaking point, where they can no longer forgive someone. Those of us who are afflicted with the disease of addiction have discovered this for ourselves, time and time again. However, the Lord has no breaking point. He knows all, and if He judges your heart true, then He shall forgive. It's incredible in its simplicity, yet it's so hard to attain, because true remorse requires one to be humbled. Faith requires diligence, and there are many challenges to that. Complacency beckons at every turn with its calm, soothing tongue. Staying strong in faith and dedication to the Lord will ensure that we can benefit from all of His goodness. On the same token, staying strong and dedicated to recovery, we can ensure that we benefit from all the goodness life in sobriety has to offer. Through the Lord this day I am reaping the benefits of both of these. So, I can declare and testify, God IS good.

Psalm 96

Psalm 96:1 says: "O <u>SING</u> unto the Lord a new song: sing unto the Lord, all the earth". A new song, such as the one I sing now. It is never too late to praise the Lord, to create anew something in His honor; much like the song that I sing through this book. I write about trials and tribulations throughout my addiction, but the underlying message is that God is doing for me now things that no one else could have before. Through a lifetime of affliction I have tried nearly every other avenue of approach to recovery. I had been dodging the Lord, or any form of religion, for that matter, as I mistakenly thought that it would have been a step in the wrong direction. Giving up my illusions of power over my world would surely leave me vulnerable to my disease. I sit in disbelief at how, by simply letting go, I have been saved! It is a miracle! Whereas, in the past, I would have turned from those who sang His praise, and run as fast as I could, I now join them; and together, we sing loud. We sing loud, because we have felt His influence in our lives, and all the greatness it has brought forth. I will watch others turn and run, as I once did. I shall not judge, for I understand all too well. But, also, I will watch some return, join hands, and join in our song. Together we will sing loud.

Psalm 97

Changing our ways in recovery is difficult. Old habits are hard to break, but changing our thoughts and perceptions proves to be an even bigger challenge. If we do not change the way we think, we are doomed to repeat the same mistakes. Psalm 97:10 says: "Ye that love the Lord, hate evil: he preserveth the souls of his saints; he delivereth them out of the hand of the wicked". Evil is something that each and every person is capable of, for we were made that way. If we do evil things, we become evil. If we do good things, we become good. But, if we are to become righteous, we must cast aside all evils. Our disease is evil. It has no place amongst the good and the righteous. It is the manifested collection of all the evils of our being. That is why we self medicate: it is too much to bear. We try to use chemicals to put our conscious mind to sleep, so that we do not have to feel as inadequate as we do. By doing this, we hand our will over to the evil, and we do evil things. We all hate this part of ourselves, which in and of itself brings us half of the way to righteousness. The other half is love for the Lord. With my love for God, and my disdain for evil, my disease has had its feet swept out from under it. The Lord is performing small miracles in me each day, and I am growing ever closer to being righteous. My evils now fear me, for I have the Lord.

Psalm 98

Psalm 98:9 says: "Before the Lord; for he cometh to judge the earth: with righteousness shall he judge the world, and the people with equity". When we hear equity we immediately think of material wealth. A house, stocks and bonds, a vehicle. But what about spiritual equity? Those who are rich in spirit reap rewards far greater than those who are wealthy financially. How many times have we heard, "money can't buy happiness"? We see the wealthy every day; but many of them are miserable, because they are poor in spirit. Pursuits of vanity have left them all but spiritually bankrupt. They pass us by on the streets with scowls on their faces; yet, we toss them a smile in return. They lose sleep at night, worrying over things they cannot bring with them when they die. We sleep soundly because we know that, when we die, we will receive spiritual riches. It is all about perspective. A righteous perspective brings us joy in this world in spite of all the other things we may lack. We can honestly be happy in our day to day lives with minimal material requirements. We are blessed with a much deeper appreciation for the things we do have, and the things we receive. We even appreciate the things we do not have, the wants that we have not been stained with. We become the grateful, the blessed, the righteous.

Psalm 99

Throughout history we can see where God has sent His chosen representatives to perform His work. Moses and his brother Aaron. King David. There were so many who had accomplished so much of the Lord's will here on earth. And to think that He has plans for even the lowliest of men, such as myself, to do works of righteousness! While I shall never be a Moses, or a David, I know that, by following His will, I can be held in the same esteem by my Lord. My purpose may be simple. Maybe it's to save just one life. Maybe it's to introduce just one person to the Lord. It could be as simple as to just <u>NOT</u> die yet. Complicated are His plans for all of us, but they're carried out with simplicity. Simple tenets have been laid before us to follow. If you read His laws, they are written so that even the simplest of minds may comprehend them. We also have tenets in recovery. And, even though most recovery groups are faith-based organizations, the tenets are written so that even the godless may recover, if they're followed. They were written this way by the forefathers of recovery because they were blessed with love for all of their brothers, and simply sought to end suffering one person at a time. Therein I find my purpose: to not cause anyone any more suffering. Instead, I am to do all that I can to heal the ailing and afflicted; for it is God's way, and it has become my own.

Psalm 100

Psalm 100:3 says: "Know ye that the Lord he is God: it is he that hath made us, and not we ourselves; we are his people, and the sheep of his pasture". I most certainly did not create myself. I did not come into this world of my own free will. I did not receive free will until I was already here. Until I found God, I had always believed that I was just a genetic combination of my parents who had grown into a diseased man. I had written off any signs of a soul within me as merely electrochemical reactions occurring within my brain, and resulting in that illusion. Science is so fascinating, and I have always loved it so. It wasn't until I found the Lord that I truly accepted that I have a soul, and I was able to see them in others. That sixth sense, as I would call it, was, in reality, my soul communing with that of another. Love, hate, desire, joy. All of these feelings are brought forth dependent upon my soul's reaction to that of another. The chemical reaction that has been shown to occur in the brain has to be triggered by SOMETHING. I believe it is the soul. Having a clean soul in recovery, I can trust my emotional reactions to things around me more than before. We know that, especially in early recovery, emotions run rampant. Mine are held in check by a soul that has been made to be wise by the will of the Lord.

Psalm 101

My actions and thoughts, from one day to the next, grow ever more satisfying to my soul. I am proud of how willingly I have accepted the Lord, for it has been long over due. I dwell not on my iniquities, for they are falling under the weight of the Lord. Psalm 101:2 says: "I will behave myself wisely in a perfect way, O when wilt thou come unto me? I will walk within my house with a perfect heart". As a recovering alcoholic, it brings me so much joy to spend every moment I can living correctly. Every second is a triumph over adversity. Every single step I take is toward becoming a better person. Where my brothers had feared my judgments in the past, they will no longer; for I have been humbled. In my eyes, where once my ego lay, they shall see nothing but kindness. All of my failings as a human being, and as a son of God, are being corrected ever so indiscreetly by the Lord. I have been made to be put on display to testify to His power. Surely, if I can change, so can any other of my afflicted brothers. Anonymity shall no longer be my disguise amongst my fellows; for my story was meant to be told. The changes in my life were meant to be witnessed. My recovery was meant to inspire; as all of ours were meant to.

Psalm 102

Success in this life has nothing to do with that in the next, with the exception of being successful in walking a righteous path. God favours the destitute; and there are none more destitute than those who have spent a lifetime battling addiction. My enemy has a name, and it is mine. My enemy has a face, and it is mine. My nemesis shares my body, my thoughts, even my soul. My undoing is never more than a momentary lapse in judgment away. There are none more destitute than us, the afflicted. Psalm 102:9 says: "For I have eaten ashes like bread, and mingled my drink with weeping". That's the life story of addiction in a single verse. But this does not need to continue until the end. Even though it may seem that we have spent eternity in addiction's cold clutches, there is hope. And though there is a lifetime of destruction, sin and vanity behind us, there IS hope. Though in the eyes of my fellows, I may seem less and broken, my hope is strong, and my prayers are pure. The path that I now walk serves to better my daily life with an increasing effect each time I wake. It also serves to guide me to the Lord, so that, when this life ends, heaven awaits. I pray that, when that day comes, I will have earned a place among God's people. But, for now, I will be mindful of each step I take; for life is good, and my heart is full.

Psalm 103

Psalm 103:3 says: "Who forgiveth all thine iniquities; who healeth all thy diseases." Forgiveness. We seek it ever so eagerly once we put down our substances. We push and pressure those we have wronged into forgiving us so we can put down the remorse we carry. But that can't be. For everyone but the Lord, it takes time and effort. We need to earn back that which we took for granted: their trust and confidence. We have to give them space, and allow them to return to us, if they so choose. The Lord forgives mercifully, if He sees that we're true of heart. Psalm 103:8 says: "The Lord is merciful and gracious, slow to anger, and plenteous in mercy". God understands better than anyone what we go through; for, even when we were blacked out or passed out, He was there. He knows all that we have done, and all that we have said. He understands we have a disease. He immediately knows whether or not we are trustworthy, for He can see straight down into our souls. Maybe this is why it has taken me so long to reach this point. Maybe the Lord saw that He couldn't trust me in those times to do His work. I wasn't ready, and I hadn't the tools. In recovery, we always say, "We all have one more run in us, but we don't know if it may be our last". By God putting his trust in me to do His work, I pray it is a sign that I am done running; because I am ever-so-weary of the drink, and ever-so-joyful in the Lord!

Psalm 104

All of the good wonders of this world have but one source. Though man may create beauty by his own hands, none can compare to the beauty that the Lord has created, long before man ever picked up his first tool. God has inspired man to create glorious works of art, and erect masterful monuments in His name. But man did not create, nor could he create, the lands, the seas, the animals that roam the wilds. Man was put here to nurture these things; for they are a gift. In much the same way we must nurture ourselves; for He created us, and placed us here. Our bodies, minds, and souls are a gift, and we must treat them accordingly. Addiction causes us to neglect all three of these. Our bodies wither to the point of a noticeable change to our loved ones. Our minds do not function properly, and we make decisions that baffle others. Our souls bear the stains of our actions, and keep us out of the Lord's favor. Sobriety is the corner stone to nurturing these things for us who are the afflicted. Our bodies, God willing, heal. Our minds are given clarity, and the quality of our decisions improve drastically. And our souls are gradually cleansed through unselfish labor and kind intentions. Ultimately we'll receive the last part of the cleansing. The Lord will touch us, even anoint us, if He so chooses. For those who have suffered, the desolate, once thought to be forsaken, we are His favorite in His employ.

Psalm 105

Psalm 105 speaks of the ten plagues in Egypt, and of the exodus to the promised land. This is a story which, for many, causes doubt in the mercy of the Lord. I know it did for me in the past, and contributed to my dismissal of my Roman Catholic upbringing. If God is so loving and kind, how could He do this? That is the question we ask ourselves, because w're passing judgment from the wrong perspective. We're seeing the oppressors as the oppressed. In reality this was all done through God's mercy for His people, to save them from their hellish lives. Perspective changes everything. That's why, in recovery, we must constantly reevaluate our perspective. If something is bothering us, try looking at it in a different way. Professionals call this "dialectical behavioral therapy". That's a fancy name for "take the negative, and reword it to be a positive". Whatever name you wish to give it, it still works. The mentality of adjusting our perspective to keep the "glass is half full" does wonders in recovery. With God, this has become ever so much easier for me. Even if I have a hard time seeing the positives in a situation, I now have tools like prayer and meditation to guide me there. These tools not only help me in this respect, but they also allow me to grow spiritually. By God, and by Him alone, I can stay positive through the darkest moments, as He has given me the proper perspective.

Psalm 106

History and our own pasts are littered with lessons. We must learn from these, so we do not repeat our mistakes, or those of others. We can use the failings of another to help guide us in our course, just as we use our own. Psalm 106 speaks of the exodus, and how the chosen people had eventually turned away from God, and invoked His wrath. Even though saved by the Lord, they had condemned themselves, by losing their gratitude, and indulging in sin. This is but a lesson to us now, more than three thousand years later; but one that can be applied to both our spirituality and to our recovery. If we turn from God, we lose His favour. I can't imagine doing that now; for He has truly shown me things that I never thought were possible. We can turn our backs on recovery; we can stop seeking treatment; we can stop reaching out when we're ailing; and we can stop sharing our cravings (also referred to as ratting out our disease). By doing this, we enable our sick minds to invoke its self-destructive wrath as it weakens our spirit and resolve. We are ill, and the disease of addiction <u>NEEDS</u> constant treatment. Treatment, as you will, comes in so many forms. Simply talking once a day with another of the afflicted can do wonders. It's free, no insurance required. And it also helps other people who struggle. Remember: it only takes two people to have a meeting. By keeping God and our recovery ahead of all other things, we will persevere. For anything we put ahead of them will surely be lost.

Psalm 107

Though society may hold us in a less desirable light, we, the afflicted and the poor, are held in God's favor. Those who have not suffered addiction, or who have not suffered through a blight of their quality of life, cannot understand. We cannot ask them to comprehend being sick, any more than they can ask us to comprehend never having been afflicted. We must keep this in mind when others may judge us unjustly. Though it may affect us directly, it is they who lack understanding; and, ultimately, it is they who have done wrong in the eyes of the Lord. It could be a lost job opportunity, being rejected by a possible romantic interest, even being cast aside by friends and family. I can't count how many times in my life I have experienced some form of rejection due to my illness. Friends in recovery have also told me many stories. I had been sober over two years and the fact that I did NOT drink was actually a deal breaker in some situations! How misguided have the so-called normal people become; when to abstain from sin is to become a social outcast? Society can keep its social standards and its opinion. I have many just brethren with which to commune; a fellowship of the righteous and of the afflicted. Better people I will not find amongst strangers. God will place in my life every person He deems I need to know. Psalm 107:10 says: "Such as sit in darkness and in the shadow of death, being bound in affliction and iron;". God alone will remove our chains to death and affliction. Society may try to bind us, but they cannot. Clean and sober and RIGHTEOUS, the afflicted cannot be bound by those who don't know the Lord.

Psalm 108

Spirituality in recovery is a must. You may not necessarily believe in God, but you need to believe in something. There is a deeper force driving the goings on about us, and we cannot overcome adversity alone. We know that our disease is more powerful than us; and no single person is more powerful than our disease. That is why it is so hard to stay sober for a loved one, such as a spouse, or even a child. It is not that they mean less to us than they should; but it's just simply the nature of the beast. For those who struggle with the concept of God, they say to use the group, or the "fellowship", as a higher power; for the combined strength of many afflicted can sometimes overpower the disease. The sense of belonging helps to alleviate the loneliness and the feelings of being cast out of society. Psalm 108:12 says: "Give us help from trouble: for vain is the help of man". Clinicians, though they may have a deep desire to help, are ultimately performing a job to provide a livelihood for themselves. Others in recovery help because it bolsters their own recovery. Though these intentions are pure, and not destructive, they do have a tinge of vanity to them. God performs His miracles within me, and gets the satisfaction of seeing me live justly. As a parent to a child who wishes to see them succeed, He gives of Himself until it is so.

Psalm 109

Psalm 109:24-25 says: "My knees are weak through fasting; and my flesh faileth of fatness. I became also a reproach unto them: when they looked upon me they shaked their heads." Though not the intent of these verses, I am reminded of how our physical appearance and our mental functions change in active addiction. It's prominent to the point where others can tell we are suffering with just a look. With rapid weight loss, and sunken cheekbones, we reek of frailty. Our attitudes change. We become both exceptionally timid, and aggressive, at the same time. We fear confrontation; but when presented with it, there is an explosion of desperate anger. We make a mess of ourselves. As we recover, we can see the reverse happening. We begin to heal physically. Our complexion returns, and our faces become full again. Life returns to us. Though in early recovery we may be emotionally fragile, we immediately begin the journey of balancing our feelings and thought processes once again. This is an experience that I've repeated many times. It's a constant cycle of varying degrees. This time, however, with God as my catalyst, I can see many of these changes occurring almost overnight, as if some outside force is acting upon me to speed me along in bouncing back. It is too obvious to ignore. My life and my mind improves by leaps and bounds from one day to the next. My faith grows with every hour, and my heart swells with every beat. I have been taken to a place where, even though I know I am diseased, I no longer SUFFER from it. It is just as much a part of me as is my arm or ear.

Psalm 110

There is something about a man of God; a presence, if you will. Even if cast among the wicked and the heathens, there is a glow about him. People may leer behind his back, jest at his expense, or judge him a fool to his face. But, deep down, there is a fear. Sometimes it's a jealousy. What if his God is real? What if He is truly righteous? What if I am wrong? Though a person may be a non-believer, to challenge a persons' faith directly is a social violation, thus condemning himself even to his fellow non-believers. Walking about with faith as an armor can cause confusion to those without faith, for they simply cannot understand. And, in a way, they <u>WANT</u> that; but they still refuse to believe. Recovery presents the same sort of challenge. Being addicted to a substance, but living day to day without actually using it, creates a glow about us. We are defeating a powerful enemy every moment of every day. Having seen us at our worst, people may become confused at seeing us at our best. They will doubt, and secretly wait for us to fail. To challenge our sobriety directly is a social violation that will ultimately cause them to be cast away by society as wicked people. Walking in sobriety as if it's an award around our neck may result in disdain; for those who have not suffered do not understand, and want us to feel shame for who we are. But secretly, to see us happy over something so simple as having spent the last 24 hours free of substances, can cause jealousy. For many, it takes much more than this to generate happiness. To see an afflicted person happy confuses the healthy. But to see an afflicted person happy brings joy to God.

Psalm 111

The laws of the Lord were given to us to use as a tool; to guide us in the correct direction, and to help us establish our societies in an upright manner. Even though the laws of man have been created by men, there is a very strong influence from the Laws of the Lord. Man has grown to hold these rules as dear as if they are his own, for they are just and true. There are also laws in recovery; rules that must be followed if we are to stay on the correct path. <u>JUST</u> don't drink; <u>JUST</u> don't use; <u>REACH</u> out for help when temptation strikes; <u>DON'T</u> isolate; and so forth. These are tried and true "recommendations" established by men who have suffered and have found recovery. I have found that, with God added to the equation, I have a set of His laws laid down before me which automatically help me embrace the rules of recovery. His guidelines are so pure that, if I follow them diligently, I cannot fail in my endeavors. Following His directions, I grow into a better person each day, adding to the previous day's lessons and learnings like building blocks. I emerge stronger, healthier, and more spiritually sound. His way makes relapse seem so far from reasonable that my disease will have to work harder than ever to convince me otherwise. The Lord keeps me safe with His guidance and strength; for my disease has grown tired under His pressure, and seeks to take a long, long slumber.

Psalm 112

The wants and desires of the wicked will perish. It is a somber truth in this world that we cannot take any of our earthly gains to the grave, nor to heaven, nor even to hell, for that matter. The only thing we can bring with us are our deeds. The way we live today determines what we are to gain tomorrow. Both the spiritual aspect, and the physical aspect of this notion, apply to recovery. In the physical realm, we can literally watch everything disappear in active addiction. Our possessions go, our health deteriorates at an alarming rate, and relationships are lost, in a horrific spiral. We forfeit our spirituality, since God has never once hidden Himself at the bottom of a bottle. While intoxication gives us the delusion of being more open-minded and closer to God, or to any higher power, it couldn't be further from the truth. We are dumping poisons into the body He gave us. We're hurting others, and are being truly selfish. We're marring our existence with a black stain of iniquity. In short, we're freely giving away all of God's great gifts because our craving for the bottle or the drugs runs so deep. Instead, I say this. Leave the bottle alone. Bask in the glory of all the fruits that life has to offer by living correctly. Let God reward us as only He can, because of living just lives. Learn to love sobriety and all the wonders it brings, more than the bottle and all the disaster that follows it. Love God, and let Him finally call the shots; for we are His, and He loves us.

Psalm 113

Psalm 113:6 says: "Who humbleth himself to behold the things that are in heaven, and in the earth!" Humbleness is the key to happiness. To truly be able to appreciate all the things we experience in life, we must approach everything with meekness. To appreciate something as simple as a tree, we cannot look at it in judgment as something less, because we can move about, and it cannot. Instead, if we humble ourselves by looking at its grand size and beauty, we begin to appreciate it. A tree does not suffer from addiction, it has never lived a self-destructive lifestyle, and it has never cast away God as a myth. It is humbling to be envious of a tree for some of its qualities. In much the same way, if we humble ourselves before God, we begin to truly appreciate Him. His qualities are unmatched, and His kindness is limitless. He has a level of mercy that no man can equal, and He can do wonders in our lives, if we'll only let Him. There is a seeming weightlessness that comes along with being humble. Worry and fear do not bear down on one who has admitted his own frailty, and does not fight it. As I humble myself, and practice mindfulness each day, I am drawn closer to the Lord. At the same time, I'm learning to truly find beauty and wonder in this world that encompasses me today; for it was put here for my use, and created by One far greater than myself.

Psalm 114

Miracles happen. Whether we attribute them to the Lord, or to something else, they do occur. Anyone who has struggled with addiction will tell you that, without a doubt, sobriety is a miracle. The disease is so powerful that fighting it seems futile. That's why, in recovery, we learn to live with the disease. We can never be cured, and we can never be "recovered"; but we can only remain in recovery. While the cravings and urges eventually go away, the potential for calamity is always present. That is why it's a miracle. To dwell with your enemy each and every single day without conflict is truly astounding. We must always acknowledge its presence, but we need not battle it. We simply tell our disease that God will not allow it to run our lives, and that <u>WE</u> are stronger with our higher power. It may seem crazy to communicate with our disease, but it is a must; for, when we leave it alone to fester, it plots and plans against us. We must constantly remind it (ourselves) that there <u>IS</u> a power greater than it, and that power is with us. In turn, we can actually <u>USE</u> our disease for a good purpose. We can help others, because we understand what they're going through. Words that fall from our mouths do not do so on deaf ears, for they are heavy with experience and hope. We can do God's work, for that is the duty of the saved yet afflicted.

Psalm 115

As I'm growing in my spirituality, I'm gaining a deeper appreciation for intangible things, like feelings, emotions, and clarity. These are things that God has gifted to me, ever since I put down the bottle and turned to Him. Psalm 115:4 says: "Their idols are silver and gold, the work of men's hands". To place value on physical items, and to compare them to spiritual advances, is not wise. Changes within ourselves cannot be purchased, and they cannot be bartered. You cannot trade money for happiness. Not true happiness. We can purchase things that give us fleeting joy, but never everlasting happiness. That comes only by changing the way we experience life, through altering our perspective. God allows me to do this, because now I have a divine Presence in my life, Who blesses me regularly, and motivates me to stay on the straight and narrow. He is a navigator, and He's incredibly easy to follow. He never leads me astray; and my faith grows with every step. As He gently pushes me in the right direction, I witness His workings ever-so-subtly around me. Things that I do not want to occur do not occur. People who challenge my stability are removed from my journey, and those who bolster it are retained and added. My pockets are full, and I have lost the desire to spend recklessly. Most importantly, I am no longer thirsty for the poison! Recovery with the Lord is a whole new experience for me; and I'm loving every minute of it.

Psalm 116

Psalm 116:15 says: "Precious in the sight of the Lord is the death of his saints". We do not want to die from our disease. We do not desire to consume toxins until we are no more; and, even when hope seems lost, deep down, we wish to endure. But, for some reason, we can't stop. The path to death is a slippery slope with no handholds in the thralls of addiction. This is not the death the Lord wants for us. Though every person who exists or has existed has/had been pre-destined to die, the self inflicted suffering was never part of the plan. Our addictions serve to challenge and teach us, to guide us away from our Lord and from ourselves. They take us to an unholy place, where we must decide if we are wicked, or emissaries of the Lord. God <u>WANTS</u> us to recover, so that we can spread these lessons. He cheers us on as we are pulled from death's clutches, and emerge, weak in body, yet strong in spirit. He watches as His groomed, afflicted saints pursue charity with a fervor ablaze. He watches His children band together to save one another. He sees us <u>SURVIVE,</u> and praise Him for His strength. Some are lost along the way; casualties of a spiritual war within. Yet many are saved. Most of all, He sees us conquer evil through His will. A more loving Father you will not find!

Psalm 117

The truth of the Lord will endure forever. Though only two verses, Psalm 117 makes a profound statement. The Lord is everlasting. As mortals who are destined to die, we cannot fathom this concept; for we were never meant to understand that while here on earth. That's why everlasting life is a gift. It's something that we strive for, and it's ultimately the greatest prize we seek. In the past, while I was wrapped up in my agnosticism, I would think of everlasting life, and dread the thought. I can see now that this was my conscious mind's way of coping with a fact that I couldn't understand, never mind that I didn't deserve. I would think of it as if being forced to continue existing against my will, when all I would crave was eternal sleep. I thought death was a really, <u>REALLY</u> long sleep. But what I had looked at as my own form of heaven was actually a hell in and of itself. To fall asleep and never wake. To never again have the joys of feeling things and interacting with things. Death seemed to be an escape; but what exactly was it that I was running from? Having spent my life playing the role of the victim, I never realized that it was <u>ME</u> who was doing the victimizing of both myself, and others. I couldn't stand myself; and death seemed to be the only escape. Now, with the Lord, and in recovery, I am once again learning to love myself. I am realizing, through God's wisdom, that I <u>DO</u> have many good qualities. I have a kindness and gentleness about me that serves to help me to help others. I have a sincerity that has been struggling to emerge. And I have faith in more than me.

Psalm 118

Psalm 118:17 says: "I shall not die, but live, and declare the works of the Lord". In turning away from alcohol, I have refused to die; refused to let myself become a statistic; refused to be a child of God who "almost" made it. I have purpose; He has plans. This is but a simple truth for me now. It's no longer just a guessing game of why I am here. The feeling of being perpetually lost has been alleviated in a single, drastic swoop. I had struggled in the past, in recovery. I spent years just not drinking. But I never really knew why, other than not wanting to die, and not wanting to fail at life. Often I would find I was only doing it for others: to make my family happy, and to make it so they wouldn't struggle with worry. But, as far as personal direction, I had none. And deep down, I wanted to drink again. So I did. All of the things I had used as motivation eventually lost their momentum in my recovery. They were gradually decelerating. God only accelerates. This is an exciting realization. Each and every day I learn something new about God, and thus learn something new about myself. From subtle to explosive, the changes are happening. Most of all I am grateful for gratefulness. It keeps me grounded and humble. Every day is a beautiful gift of growth and joy. As Psalm 118:24 says: "This is the day which the Lord hath made; we will rejoice and be glad in it".

Psalm 119

I was introduced to the Lord because I was ill. In the beginning, I saw this as an act of desperation, as I would assume many who know me would, as well. It has not taken long for me to see what the true reason this occurred was. I needed God! Illness brought me to Him, but my heart drove me to accept Him. By turning to the Lord, I had opened a floodgate of spiritual experiences that I had been forsaking my entire life. As long as I follow His precepts, I will reap the rewards of being a better person for the rest of my days. Though I am still, and will always be, ill, the Lord is not allowing me to suffer. What has happened in my life, even just recently, is astounding. The people that have been sent to help me, and who have turned out for support; the saints among men who care for me as a son and a brother; the mere acquaintances who have revealed that they care for me deeply. This is God working through good people to reach out and help me. He has angels hidden among us, ready to take up arms against evil to protect His children. I see now that it is my destiny to join their ranks, and fight the wickedness of this world, standing by their sides. Psalm 119:71 says: "It is good for me that I have been afflicted; that I might learn thy statutes." I met Him because I was ill. I love Him because he does not let me feel ill.

Psalm 120

Psalm 120:6 says: "My soul hath long dwelt with him that hateth peace". My disease hates peace. It yearns for the constant struggle, the battle within, for control. A raging war of epic proportions is occurring every moment behind seemingly peaceful eyes. Those who have not experienced it cannot see it. They see a drunk or an addict who has finally managed to stop; seemingly at peace, because the toxins are gone. When the fog of intoxication lifts, it is the fog of war that settles into the field. The battle wakes us up in the middle of the night, our subconscious dreaming of relapse. And even though it's just a dream, we awake with very <u>REAL</u> guilt. We constantly analyze comments and situations again and again, trying to decide if they were directed at our shortcomings. Beasts from the darkness gallop at full speed across the plains of our minds, all day and all night, searching for the weakest point in our willpower stronghold; and taunting us. We have a stockpile of motivators we use to keep them at bay: sponsors, fellowships, loved ones, treatment. Unfortunately, these are exhaustible resources. The Lord is never exhausted. And with Him, I do not awake in the middle of the night with guilt. The fields of my mind are at peace. No beasts. No fog. For the first time in my life there is peace, and there is quiet. You can hear the birds, and smell the fresh fields that are not stained with war nor rot. The sun shines, and the walls remain strong. There may be a day when the war returns to this field, but I will be ready; for I have the best defense: He Who has created it all!

Psalm 121

Psalm 121:3 "He will not suffer thy foot to be moved: he that keepeth thee will not slumber". God never rests, and tends dutifully to His responsibilities as the Lord. His mercy is unwavering. His work is everlasting, and He conducts it each and every moment with love for us. He watches over me, not only while I'm awake, but when I sleep, as well. My subconscious mind has been freed of plaguing thoughts throughout my sleep. When we sleep in recovery it can be a dangerous place. We have powerful dreams brought forth by our disease, for it remains ever so active while we slumber. We remember them in the morning, and it causes very real emotional responses that threaten to weaken our spirits throughout the day. This is how clever and vigilant the disease of addiction is. It even works while we sleep; which is yet another sign of how much more powerful it is than our conscious minds. With God as my bedside Protector, I sleep soundly. Shackled by my faith in the Lord, the disease of addiction does not have the ability to trounce about in my head when I am vulnerable. The Lord protects me, His son, in my times of trouble, and in my moments of weakness. I fear not the evenings. I do not fear my bed. I lay down at the time of rest with a full heart and an empty mind, and awake at dawn with the same. God has blessed me, so that my enemy may not reign over any part of my existence; for that is a right that I have given freely to the Lord, and to the Lord alone.

Psalm 122

I was brought to the Lord by the guides He had sent to me under the guise of everyday people. Psalm 122:1 says: "I was glad when they said unto me, let us go into the house of the Lord". Though returning to God after a life of sin and destruction had seemed a daunting endeavour, I was relieved at how easy a transition it was. I merely had to be humble, and honest. The disease of addiction has the power to enfeeble us; and, with God's grace, leave us humbled in our meekness. It is from this place that we can begin to rebuild and thrive. It is from this place that we can find peace at last; a peace that we want to share with others whom we see struggling. Psalm 122:8 says: "For my brethren and companions' sakes, I will now say, peace be within thee". To aid another in recovery is to help bring them peace. It is when we are at peace with ourselves that we then become able to help another who is struggling. And they, in turn, may help another, and so on. The possibilities for healing are endless; like the domino effect. All it takes is that first person to topple the first piece, and the others will follow. I pray that, with this book, and through my life's remaining journeys, I may topple many of the first pieces in a line of healings. However, even if it's just one, I will have served my purpose here.

Psalm 123

As we try to walk a righteous path, and live life in a healthy manner, we will face oppressors. These can be people or things that will confront us head on in our journey, and attempt to slow or halt our progress. Sometimes these things can't be stopped, and these people may not even be aware of the threat they are imposing. This is where being mindful, and letting God guide you, will come into play. It could be something as simple as a promotion at work. While it may seem to the employer they are helping and/or rewarding us, they could be doing harm. There may be additional stress that we do not need that comes with the new title. We could simply be happier where we currently are. We may not feel comfortable with the new situations. We have to be mindful of how we feel about all of the changes in our lives; for, in one way or another, they will all impact our sobriety. As I let God guide me, I have learned to listen to His words. He lets me know, when I face these decisions, which way to turn, through feelings. Though I am working on speaking up and voicing my thoughts, I still have so much to learn. I have noticed that, at times, when I have failed to confront ill changes, out of fear of refusal, God sends someone to do it for me. He defends my sobriety as fiercely as I <u>SHOULD</u>. And from this, I learn.

Psalm 124

The Lord is on our side. He stands behind us, along with those who love us on this earth. God wants to see us succeed, as do all the others who value us in their lives. There are many people who feel the impact of our addictions. We abuse them, and hurt them; for it is the wrath of our demons that they face when they try to help. Yet, when we finally exit the stupor, and reach back out, not all have left. Some have, being weary; and all of them are skeptical at best. Some will never return, and some rush to our sides as if we had only taken a brief stumble. We may mourn the relationships that have been lost, but we cannot dwell on them. We cherish the relationships that endure, and we must continue in them with meekness as they are repaired. However, our relationship with God is one that can be fixed immediately. Humbled, repentant, honest, we become the forgiven, and once again the favored. His mercy knows no limits, if we stay true and faithful. Kindness will rain down upon us equal to that which we give to others. Though at times we may seem doomed to repeat the same mistakes, yet, through hope and prayer, there is salvation. Never lose hope, pray often, and ask to be relieved of mortal vanities that ultimately drag us down. Fear the Lord. Don't fear His wrath, for His mercy runs deeper. But, fear His absence. Though God is everywhere, we can feel His absence when we cast Him aside. Our substances seek to control our gift of free will and undermine God. With His strength, I have the power to never pick up that first drink. I have the power of prayer. I have enough control over my free will to hand it over to God. And, I <u>AM</u> sober.

Psalm 125

God, Who is so infinitely powerful and wise, has given us the ability to make bad decisions, and to do wrong things. He could have easily made us to all be pure hearted, and have eliminated our earthly struggles; but, then, where would the free will be? God is not in the business of making robots; no, not His chosen people. Without struggle there would be no lessons, no learning. After coming out of active addiction, it is important that we look back on our use, and study it, rather than loathe it. What lessons can we take away? What can we learn from our sufferings? If we can learn, then it has not all been in vain! We can give it purpose in our lives, and let it make us better! Though we will surely find no beauty or admiration in our past of active addiction, we can surely find some new tools to prevent it in the future. We may even be able to find God . . . But surely, we all, at one point, have said, "If I just didn't go there", or, "if I had only avoided that person". These are lessons that we all needed to learn. What's happened has happened. Learn from it, and let it go as fast as you can. Surely, if the Lord can forgive us, then we can learn to forgive ourselves. Do not dwell on the lessons, and do not review those events over and over, which are resentments. Through practice we can learn how to do this on a regular basis in our lives; even regarding things that have nothing to do with our recovery. With God guiding my thought processes, this is becoming common practice in my life every day; and I rejoice.

Psalm 126

The disease of addiction, if left unchecked, threatens to hold us captive. Psalm 126:4 says: "Turn again our captivity, O Lord, as the streams in the south". What a wretched and ironic captivity: to be locked away within our own minds, as the demons take control of our bodies. We move about in pursuit of our sinful obsessions, powerless to stop them. We are forced to bear witness to the horrors that we do, and those that stream from our mouths. We watch helpless as we strike down the ones we love. Often, when we awake in a moment of semi-sober clarity, we will see what we have done. We see, and in disgust we crawl back to our disease and allow it to again take over, begging it: "Please, I do not wish to see what I have done, take this pain away, make me forget". How absurd to look for salvation by clinging to the one holding us down. With God in my life, I am no longer a captive. I'm no longer bound and held down. I nevermore look TO my enemy for relief FROM my enemy. The Lord holds my enemy captive now; locked away deep in a dark place, where there is no light in which to make plans for its next hostile takeover. God stands vigilant guard over my soul, for He has laid claim to it. Free from the bonds of a spiritual battle I would never have won alone, I rub my wrists; for they are sore from the shackles. God relieves me of the suffering, and sets me free in the world as a new man; a man of God, a man of goodness and peace.

Psalm 127

To labor throughout the day on vain things does not feed the spirit, even though, for many of us, this is a necessity, to acquire the means to survive, and to perform our spiritual duties. We may work for companies, and all companies have a bottom line. They seek to profit from our labor, and, in turn, they compensate us for our work. The compensation they provide allows us to acquire necessities like food and shelter. However, here is the point where we must make a spiritual decision: Do we use our earnings to acquire vain things, or do we use it for a deeper purpose? Charity is cleansing to the soul. It can be as simple as giving a couple cans of food to the needy, or even giving our time to someone who needs it. It could be lending a hand to a friend, or providing an ear to someone who is suffering. There is no end to the things we can do to help others. To give of ourselves, when it would be much easier to simply keep for ourselves, is doing the Lord's work. As we recover from addiction and the lifestyle that accompanied it, it is incredibly therapeutic to give to others. It makes us feel good, it helps rebuild our sense of self-worth; and, ultimately, it is GOD'S work! It is an all-around winning situation from which everyone benefits; and, more importantly, no one is hurt. To become charitable, in spite of the person we once were, is to truly enter into the Lord's way, and into a deeper existence here on earth.

Psalm 128

By following God's path, we can reap the rewards of living a good life. These rewards will not be what we once sought in our past. It will not be riches or vain possessions, for these are brought unto us by our own hands. Instead, it will be the blessing of peace. I cannot describe the level of peace and acceptance that I have already achieved this time in sobriety. The guilt, shame, and fear that usually lasts for months and months has vaporized right before me. With God, I am reaping the blessings of a clear mind. I do not struggle with self-loathing and remembrances of sorrow. Instead, I am filled with joy for the moment, and promise for the future. My heart swells as I ponder the thought of living out the rest of my days in this manner. Could there really have been a peace so profound and deep that I had been shunning all this time? God reminds me every day that it is never too late to seek out this blessing, and to share that knowledge with my fellows. By casting aside our armor of proof and facts and confirmations, our eyes will truly be opened. Through faith, we learn to see the real goings on about us. We learn to see into the very souls of others. The kindred of spirit are drawn to one another as magnets, and, together, we prosper in all of our blessings.

Psalm 129

Realizing that I have been an alcoholic since I was born helps to put my disease in perspective. Though I was in my teens before I ever picked up my first drink, I have always had alcoholic tendencies. Alcoholism is an obsession with alcohol. There are many things in my life that I can look back on, and honestly say that I approached them with an alcoholic's mentality. Moderation has never been one of my strengths. The "all or nothing" approach that had earned me so many successes in my life had also become my undoing. I would attack any goal with such a relentless ambition that I would not, could not, stop, until either it was accomplished, or sheer exhaustion took over. In the same manner, my drinking could not stop until it was arrested by some outside force, or I simply could no longer stay conscious. We, in recovery, often look back to our youth, and wonder where we went wrong; where the "switch" had finally been thrown, and we became ill. It is when we realize that the switch has always been on that we can truly start to heal. It is, to put it plainly, simply part of who we are. This is a piece of the sobriety puzzle where I find God is extremely helpful. By humbling myself, and by admitting to myself and others that I have always been somewhat "broken", I am relieved of it. I no longer carry it, and no longer need to waste time trying to evaluate my past. Reminiscing can be spiritually exhausting. God has asked me to accept it, and to move on. So I have. There are more important things to be tended to.

Psalm 130

We are taught in recovery that we can not isolate. We need to share how we feel, share when we get cravings, and keep others involved in our recovery. The last thing we want is the "I can do this alone" mentality. I know, from personal experience, that this is often quite difficult; especially once we have consciously or subconsciously decided to drink or use. Our disease is in full swing at this point, and implores us not to reach out. We become laser-focused on one thing: our substance; and we are all but lost. We will hear many people describe this state of mind as almost trance-like, sublime, a near out-of-body experience. We go out, acquire our substance, and use as if on autopilot. That is how powerful the disease is. It begins to flood our brains with pleasure chemicals like dopamine at the mere idea of using again. Addiction is very clever. So, at these times, when our phones may weigh 1000 pounds, and we can't look anyone in the eyes, let alone telling them how we feel, then, are we damned to battle this alone? Not if we have God. We can speak to the Lord any time we wish, without even having to open our mouths. And the best part is, He ALWAYS listens. Before taking the ride to the liquor store or to the dealer, talk to God for a minute. Ask for help and guidance. Maybe just tell Him how we're feeling. You would be surprised by the miracles that can happen, simply by praying. I can testify to that.

Psalm 131

Psalm 131:1 says: "Lord my heart is not haughty, nor mine eyes lofty: neither do I exercise myself in great matters, or in things too high for me". This verse leads me to my favorite coping skill: keep it simple! As the serenity prayer says: "Please, God, grant me the serenity to accept the things I CANNOT CHANGE, the courage to change the things I can, and the wisdom to know the difference". It's so easy in life to get all wrapped up in things that are so far beyond our reach that it is utterly fruitless to even try. In recovery, this can be deadly! Keep it simple; one day at a time; don't sweat the small stuff. Whatever slogan works for you, hold on to it; for it can be a lifesaver. Lofty goals can be enticing, for they give us the illusion of purpose in a world where we may otherwise feel lost. But, in reality, we're setting ourselves up for failure; because, when we fail to achieve them, or fail to make change happen, or simply do not feel that we've progressed far enough, we damage ourselves spiritually. In a way, we let ourselves down; and that is not how we should ever feel about ourselves. Live life from one day to the next, especially in recovery, and take things as they come. Goals are great, for they keep us going in one direction instead of twenty. But set REASONABLE ones. God would never ask us to do something unreasonable, for that is not how He works. His reason is flawless. I have come to find that, if I simply allow God to set my goals for me, I will walk a level road the rest of my days.

Psalm 132

Psalm 132:1 says: "Lord, remember David, and all his afflictions:". Though this Psalm speaks of king David (and, in my opinion, is it coincidence that we share the name?) it still strikes me. As I read through the Psalms, I have found many places where it is as if God is trying to speak to me, and to remind me that He has a place for me in His purposes. Growing up, I had always been told that my father gave me a holy name; for David was a holy man; but I thought, simply, that my father had named me after himself, though not calling me a junior. It wasn't until I read the Bible the first time that I understood the importance my name played in the beginning of things. However, being agnostic, it held no real value. Now, as I look again at my faith with an open mind and a full heart, I can't help but feel a kinship with king David. It's not simply through sharing a name; but it's also by both being afflicted. Even David, in his youth, reminds me of myself: ever ready to tend to the flock, though it wasn't the most glamourous job that needed to be done. Also, we have both endured struggles, being seen as family outcasts; for David was not the first-born, and I am an alcoholic. The feeling that God is speaking to me through the book is such an amazing realization. The thought that I could one day be held in similar esteem as David in the heavens is breathtaking, almost overwhelming!

Psalm 133

Finding my inner peace with the help of God has helped me to find peace with others. I can live amongst my fellows, and be content with the relationships that I've formed, because I am content with myself. As the old saying goes: we must learn to love ourselves before we can love another. I find this to be very true. If you simply cannot bear to be yourself, how could you possibly find value in, or appreciate, another? If you can not treat yourself right, how would you know how to treat another? I know that, when I wasn't happy with myself, I would take it out on others; sometimes subtly, other times not so much. That is, in no way, a spiritual lifestyle. I would disguise my inner resentments toward myself with humor and avoidance; using every opportunity that presented itself to divert attention away from me and my illness. As I move forward in life now, open and honest about my powerlessness, I find that I hold no resentments against myself. God has removed all of these; for they ate away at my spirituality like a corrosive. He has left me spiritually sound; and, in doing so, has allowed me to look upon my brothers and sisters with a fondness I've never before felt. I see many good people in my daily life, <u>INCLUDING</u> myself; and that is something that most surely is a gift from God.

Psalm 134

I pray to the Lord in thanks several times each day, for I am truly grateful. Where I once counted my sufferings and curses, I now count my blessings. It is amazing the change in mind set when you start to focus solely on the positives in life. To be an optimist in today's world is truly a challenge; and being an optimistic alcoholic in today's world is nearly impossible. When we look to God for answers, He has this miraculous way of telling us exactly what we need to hear at the exact moment that we need to hear it. I have had this happen on so many occasions that I cannot help but feel hopeful that tomorrow will continue to bring me growth and happiness in the same way that today has. Falling asleep at night with nothing but a grateful mind serves to strengthen my soul. I do not dread the next day, nor do I curse the last. Every moment of the day that I enjoy is a gift. Every moment throughout the day that I do not enjoy is a gift that helps me to better appreciate the enjoyable ones. This is optimism put into practice. I could never function on this level before I accepted the Lord. This seemingly simple perspective change has done wonders for my recovery, and has made sobriety a real pleasure. Finding the ever-elusive happiness without our substance is incredibly daunting; but God has shown me the way. Through Him I have found that which before I had thought was impossible. I have found my inner grateful self.

Psalm 135

In life, we often find ourselves assigning too much value to unimportant things. In addiction, we find ourselves placing immense value in horrible things. Ask anyone who has ever tried to take away an alcoholic's bottle. Enter an alcoholic's or an addict's abode, and you're likely to see exactly what we value in active addiction. It's a veritable fortress of solitude. The doors are locked, the blinds are drawn, and the windows are closed. Darkness is about, even at mid-day. There is clutter and foul odors, and untended chores have left piles of laundry and dishes. This is the environment in which we exist; the spawning pool in which our disease wallows in joy and flourishes. We value these things because it feeds our feelings of worthlessness and self-pity. These, in turn, give us justification to continue drinking or using. They all play back into the one thing that we value most: our substance. Clear the mind and sober the spirit, and our values change. We value cleanliness and upright-ness, sometimes to the point of over-compensating for how we had lived in the past. We may also learn to value ego, whereas we used to be full of self-pity. We must be mindful of this. Either of these extremes are very hazardous to our well-being. We, as diseased people who wish to live happy lives, need to remain humble! God keeps me ever-so-humble by His pres-ence alone. That is a blessing, for it renders me im-mune to delusions of grandeur, and keeps me mindful of the fact that I am weak. I was never able to find this perfect balance, until I let God into my life. He has shown me exactly where to set my eyes: on Him.

Psalm 136

The meek shall inherit the earth. For those who don't pursue a righteous life, they'll acquire many temporary things. Upon death, the suffering ones are risen to God, and He shall judge us justly. The important part is to stay on the path of greatness. This path is not one to take us through a life of monumental accomplishments or material gains. It was designed by the Lord to shape our spirit, and to mold it into something great. The financially poor tend to be richer spiritually. Who is truly richer: the man who is grateful for a warm bed at night, or the man who is grateful for the fancy new car? Sobriety itself can be cunning. At times, we assume that, if addiction is wrong, and sobriety is right, then there should be opposite occurrences in each. In addiction we became homeless, so in recovery we must acquire a new home. In addiction we lost possessions, so in recovery we must accumulate them. While this train of thought appears correct, we must make sure it is directed appropriately. It is our spirit and value systems that need to be turned around. We have to value the things that we lost in addiction: like clarity, stability, reliability, spirituality, honesty, etc. Once we learn to do this, we become truly rich of spirit, and, believe it or not, happy. Other things, material things, come and go. But training ourselves to be great of mind and spirit will last forever. Allowing God to show us the way makes this easy.

Psalm 137

It is important in recovery to remember that there will be setbacks. It is just a fact of life here on earth. Be it a tragedy, a loss, a relapse, these things may eventually occur. The critical part is to not give up! Though at times it may seem that all is lost, that we have become forsaken, we must look within and ask ourselves: "Have I done wrong"? Ask God to show you. If the answer is "no", then persevere! Things always have a way of turning out okay, as long as we keep the faith and do not give up on ourselves, or on God. If the answer is "yes", then pray for guidance! Human beings are far from perfect. Our faults are part of the building materials that were used to construct us. There is no shame in not being perfect. The only shame is in pretending that we <u>ARE</u>. God wants us to recover, to love Him and each other, and to spread peace and joy in any way we can. Through His gift of free will to us and others, we are left vulnerable to troubles. Don't confuse them with being forsaken. For though it may not have been His will that put us in ill positions, His will can surely pull us free from them. Prayer is a powerful tool. Pray often. Pray loud or pray soft; for, regardless, God hears them the same. Speak to Him frequently, and you may find, as I have, that He answers exactly when you need Him to.

Psalm 138

Psalm 138:3 "In the day when I cried Thou answeredst me, and strengthenedst me with strength in my soul". Though it has not been very long since I finally cried out to the Lord for salvation, it seems almost a lifetime ago. The Lord has a miraculous way of wiping clean the past - even that of a heretic. As I try to look back to before the Lord entered my life, it is as if a fog has been lowered and makes it hazy to my eyes. I no longer fully understand the mind set I had before. I truly believe that this is God's doing. I have acknowledged that it was wrong and asked for it to be taken away, and it has. This gives me much hope for the future, since I have so easily been accepted by Him, powerless and humble as I ought to be. He has strengthened me by removing many of my downfalls. The things I need and want have changed drastically, and they are truer than before. I crave peace and love, and steer away from tumultuous endeavours. Most importantly, I do not crave alcohol. I know that, should I take a sip, I would surely be lost to the wolves. Without sobriety, I would lose all of these gifts from God; for my disease seeks to make me blind to Him. Fortunately, for my own sake, the will of God and the will of my disease are two entirely different forces. My God is much stronger than my disease. So, may His will be done, and may His will be mine.

Psalm 139

Psalm 139:23-24 says: "Search me, O God, and know my heart: try me, and know my thoughts: and see if there be any wicked way in me, and lead me in the way everlasting". Spiritual growth is a lifelong endeavour. Much like addicts and alcoholics can never be fully "recovered", neither can we be perfectly righteous, nor perfectly spiritual. We can only continue to progress in our relationships with God. To simply say "I'm there", and to stop craving spiritual development, is to essentially give up. We were never intended to be able to perfectly interpret the Lord's Word, nor His will, for that would require His perfection. It is the thirst, the yearning to pursue the deeper meaning to His plans, that keeps us of a righteous heart. To look to God each day with the inquisitive eyes of a child is beautiful. Teach me, please teach me, and guide me. Show me something new today, so that I may grow wiser in righteous things. The day I wake and I do not wish to learn anything that the Lord has to offer is a day I truly need to pray; for that's a sign that I could be in spiritual distress. In relation to recovery, we must practice the same thing. The day we wake, and we do not ask ourselves, "What can I do to better strengthen my recovery today?", is a day to pray, a day to call support, go to a meeting, or to meditate on our recovery. The day we wake, and feel that we have grown enough in recovery or spirituality, is a dark day. Pray for humbleness, pray for hunger for the Word, and pray to return to the path.

Psalm 140

Faith in the Lord, and thus in ourselves, to do the next right thing, is a powerful force in our recovery. If we can't trust ourselves, then we truly sleep with the enemy each and every night. I had never fully trusted myself in my past attempts at recovery. Years of "just don't drink" ultimately led me back to alcohol. Looking back, I can understand now that I never fully trusted myself to make correct decisions. I attribute this in part to the lack of God in my life. I refused to acknowledge Him, so I never was graced with the feeling that I was being guided in my actions. I was guiding myself, and I was all too familiar with how imperfect and frail I was. Psalm 140:12 says: "I know that the Lord will maintain the cause of the afflicted, and the right of the poor". Have faith that, by accepting God, He will be an influence in our lives. He will guide our thoughts and actions, and protect us through dire straits. There is no longer a need to second guess each and every choice I make, because I know that, in my glorious imperfectness I am not alone. I am the poor, I am the afflicted, I am the grateful, I am the kind. I see the Lord, and I am blessed to be able to say that. I no longer fear to trust in myself, because God has blessed me. He does not bless the wicked, nor the heathen. Therefore, I stand in His favour, and I wish to stand nowhere else.

Psalm 141

Psalm 141:4 says: "Incline not my heart to any evil thing, to practise wicked works with men that work iniquity: and let me not eat of their dainties". With a deeper appreciation and respect for a world that is filled with God, I find myself progressively less tempted by things that used to pull me in as if they had their own gravity. I yearn not to socialize with any who do evil things, and have a deeper love for those who do good in their lives. I have made new friends and acquaintances who are wholesome. If we are to be successful, recovery requires us to do these things. We act upon what our values are, and if we do not value good things, then we will not act in a good manner. We must remove from our foresight all the things that will threaten our healing. God has promised that, if we adhere to His Word, and live correctly, we will know the meaning of true happiness. We'll find peace amongst turmoil, and we shall reap His blessings a-plenty. These small changes that I must make in my life are but a meager sacrifice for all that I am to receive in return. Even today, as I live contented be-yond measure, simply reading His Word and knowing that I'm walking a good path today, fills me with joy. There is nothing I need to go out and acquire to make this moment any better or more rewarding. I feel my reward all around me, at all times.

Psalm 142

Psalm 142:6 says: "Attend unto my cry; for I am brought very low: deliver me from my persecutors; for they are stronger than I." Surely my disease wishes to persecute me, and it is most certainly stronger than I am. In the past, I had tried to use the fellowship and my sponsor as my higher power. I felt that, with their support, I was finally strong enough to overcome my illness. This method does work for many a recovering alcoholic who has yet to find God. It worked for me for years; but, ultimately, I hadn't become strong enough. Though I had become more resilient and resistant to my alcoholism, I was not above it; for it knows me all too well, since it is part of me. With God as my Higher Power, I am truly amazed at the things He is doing for me! How utterly relieved I am of all the suffering associated with my disease. How refreshed my mind is, and how strong my body is becoming. Flesh returns to my bones, because I am once again healthy. I smile quite often, because my mind is clear of all the wicked debris. I do not suffer through fear or anger or hate or even guilt. Instead, I look no more than a few moments into the future, and keep myself grounded in the moment, staying present and mindful of my Higher Power. I must be receptive and ready to hear His voice when He speaks; and He has made me strong.

Psalm 143

As children of God, and those that seek to follow a righteous journey, we are blessed with a powerful tool. We have the right to turn to God for answers when we are struggling. The wicked and the evil doers do not have this privilege, for God does not deal in their ways. This blessing is so prevalent to me, because, in the past, I have attempted to endure every struggle on my own, and to find the answers by myself. But I failed to do so more often than not. Thus, a lack of resolution in my troubles would ultimately lead to resentments, which drained my happiness away. God now guides me speedily toward resolutions when I am confronted with troubles. He knows, even better than I, that resentments are deadly to those with addictions. He has stepped in and touched me, so that I need no longer struggle within the resentment vortex. Resentments, as the word dissected stands as re-sentiments, is the process of reliving an event over and over again; of dwelling on the past, and keeping us away from the present. It's a circular thinking pattern, that keeps us stuck in our darkest moments, and steals away our strength. As someone in recovery, and someone who has failed at recovery in the past, I can testify that, indeed, resentments are the number one offender. My solution to this is the Lord. He has already relieved me of even the freshest regrets, and continues to bless and bandage some of the oldest, so they may finally heal.

Psalm 144

Ask, and you shall receive - but you <u>MUST</u> ask! If you come to the Lord humbled, yet spiritually strong and faithful, He will hear your words. Ask Him not for vain things, and He will hear your cries. He will answer your call, and though there may be no lightning or thunder or divine flood as evidence, it has not fallen on deaf ears. At the same time, we can turn to our fellows in recovery for help in our time of need; but we <u>MUST</u> reach out to them! They cannot read our minds, and they cannot see into our souls. We have to take the first step, and humble ourselves in our powerlessness. We hear many sponsors or friends say, "Call me <u>BEFORE</u> you use, but don't bother after you pick up, because I can't help you then". Just as we cannot ask the Lord to grant us vanity, we cannot ask our fellows in recovery to endure us in active addiction. To help others arrest it before it manifests itself <u>IS</u> the purpose of recovery. It's for us to get well, and then to help another who struggles with addiction, through our experience, guidance, and support. We can only keep sobriety by giving it away. We can only stay healthy by healing others. We can only understand the pains and fears of someone if we have cried with them. Together, we unite against a common enemy; and, praise be to God, we shall be victorious!

Psalm 145

Praise be to God for all the beauty of my life. Let me sing it unto Him and shew forth my gratefulness. Where I once wallowed in the valley of strife and inner turmoil, I now walk amongst good men, and achieve greater spirituality with each step. I fear not to look in the eyes of another, for I have no shame that causes me to drag my eyes to my feet. The Lord has alleviated these things, and granted me an inner peace, where I'm now able to focus on beauty, both in the world around me, and within myself. I have an inner beauty, a kind and gentle spirit that has been yearning to be seen. Locked away for so long by the demons within, the Lord has brought it back out into the light, and it's flourishing there. I desire to share it with all whom I may cross paths. Simple smiles from strangers when I approach them with kindness light up my days. Associates who struggle and hear my kind words of encouragement seem to raise up, and my heart swells. Those who have been appointed over me panic when they fear they have upset me, and I ease that panic with kindness and they are relieved. Oh, how drastic are the changes and perceptions, once God is allowed to influence. His impact on my life is spilling forth onto others as I act in a way that God would want me to. I see this as part of His plan and my actions are following through on it. I am guided by His power.

Psalm 146

Psalm 146:8 says: "The Lord openeth the eyes of the blind: the Lord raiseth them that are bowed down: the Lord loveth the righteous". How often in life can we say that we are the favorite, though we have so many issues? Usually it would be the opposite. This just goes to show how far society's perceptions have strayed from the Lord's. Society does not treasure the ill, the poor, the lost. We serve as little more than statistics to quote in financial meetings. Even our own families avoid us, because we represent too much pain and suffering to be borne. But they fail to see our strengths, for they believe we have none. Some of the strongest people I have ever met were in recovery. They could talk for two hours non-stop and keep me hanging on every word. They were brilliant, strong, motivating people. They hold high places in society; but many of their fellows have no clue that they are the afflicted. A sheep amongst wolves. Yet, they still go to speak at treatment centers, they go to meetings, and they help complete strangers do God's work. To become addicted does not mean someone is broken. It is a disease of the mind, and it does <u>NOT</u> have to kill us. Through God, fellowships, treatment, and practice the disease is entirely manageable. As a diabetic needs insulin regularly, so too, the addicted needs medicine. They don't need pills nor injections, but, rather heavy doses of hope and faith. This is nearly one of the only diseases that, while incurable, still can be arrested completely by happiness.

Psalm 147

The healing powers of the Lord stretch far beyond the limits of earthly medicine. It transcends the physical and mental level of revival that man has accomplished. We have learned to replace hearts, mend depression, even repair damaged minds. However, there is no hospital one can go to which can repair the soul. Throughout my life of addiction, I attended innumerable treatment programs, and more meetings than I can ever possibly remember. Professional treatment was always pretty much the same, with the same literature, and the same teachings. Yet I always went back, because I was hoping that, one day, I would find what was missing. However, I had no clue what it was, and no idea where to start looking. Could there have been a simple statement that would suddenly make everything so clear? Maybe it would be a miraculous medication that would make me feel happy again, or possibly a clinician who could finally reach my sick mind and mend it. However this was not the case. While I am grateful for all those professional and personal acquaintances who tried so valiantly, they just simply did not have the power to make a change within me. Only I had that power, and it started with turning to God. He is the only one who is stronger than my disease. Where man had failed over and over again, He triumphed in just a moment! I have found what was missing. I had just been looking in all of the wrong places.

Psalm 148

I stand in utter awe of Him. I was humbled, and came to Him, weeping and tending my wounds. When He made Himself known to me, I became even more humbled. To feel His grand presence, and to feel His workings from within my very soul, was overwhelming! With a power so great, He is the only one who has ever stood nose to nose in defiance of my addiction. In the course of hours He smote a lifetime of wrongs. He cleansed my entire slate purely by His will. I was left reeling and I scrambled to pray to Him, to say, "Thank You"! Remorse gripped me tightly; not because of my addiction, or for the evils I had done, for He had removed these already. I was remorseful for my actions against Him. And thus, I was humbled further. My guides told me to let it go, that God had already forgiven me, and I tried. It was hard, because I had become accustomed to apologizing to those I had wronged, and receiving half-hearted skeptical acceptances of those apologies. However, the Lord does not deal in half-heartedness. He has mercy that I could never comprehend. He loves deeper than I ever could. I know he has forgiven me, and I no longer live with remorse. This does not mean I do not acknowledge that I did wrong in the past; but it simply means that I do not dwell there.

Psalm 149

Psalm 149:4 says: "For the Lord taketh pleasure in his people: He will beautify the meek with salvation". It amazes me how I have lived my entire life trying to create an image of strength and success around me. I wanted others to look at me, and to see a strong, intelligent, gifted man. I joined the Army very young. Surely they would think me strong. I learned many things: tricks and puzzles. Surely they would think me intelligent. I worked hard and bought nice, flashy things. Surely they would think me gifted. In the end I lay broken, weak, dumb, and poor. My ill pursuits left me diseased and fallen. Today, I can say with a smile, that I am weak. I am only a man, and I am an alcoholic. I am frail, I lack knowledge, and, until recently, I did not know what a true gift was. And, I am an alcoholic. I <u>AM</u> the meek, the poor, the cast out, the alcoholic! And I wouldn't have it any other way. In a way, I feel as if God has already beautified me; not in vain respects, but, rather, that I can actually look at myself in the mirror without sorrow. The place I had gone, where my own image displeased me, was such a sad place. Now I look, and I see a servant of the Lord. A holy man under the disguise of a 34-year-old blue-eyed brown-haired alcoholic. I'm proud to be an afflicted one living sober. I'm proud to be a messenger for God. And I'm proud to be able to help save another of God's chosen people; the meek ones.

Psalm 150

As I am at the end of the Psalms, I read of praise for the Lord. I am truly grateful for His presence in my life. He has brought to me so many gifts in such a short time; gifts that allow me to finally feel at home in sobriety, and, more importantly, in my own skin. Without Him, I would surely continue to be lost in a world where I felt I did not belong. He has gifted me with a soundness of mind, a steady hand, and true sight that no longer veers to the darkness. He, and He alone, has the power to bring me back from the depths. He, and He alone, has saved my soul. Praise be to the Lord. May I forever be in Your favour.

God has made me grateful for many things, and has sent me angels throughout my life to protect and watch over me, until I found my purpose. Without them, this book would not have been possible. I would like to thank them now.

To Scott and Jacqui: My guardian angels, whom the Lord sent to see me well, and kindly introduce me to Him. For he had decided it was time.

To my parents, David and Marlyn: You have endured much at the hands of my addiction. May this book bring you hope that you no longer need to worry about your son.

To my brother, Daniel: You are the strongest man I know.

57524763R00088

Made in the USA
Charleston, SC
15 June 2016